WEAPON

FAIRBAIRN-SYKES COMMANDO DAGGER

LEROY THOMPSON

Series Editor Martin Pegler

OSPREY PUBLISHING
Bloomsbury Publishing Plc

Kemp House, Chawley Park, Cumnor Hill, Oxford OX2 9PH, UK
29 Earlsfort Terrace, Dublin 2, Ireland
1385 Broadway, 5th Floor, New York, NY 10018, USA
Email: info@ospreypublishing.com
www.ospreypublishing.com

OSPREY is a trademark of Osprey Publishing Ltd

First published in Great Britain in 2011

A catalog record for this book is available from the
British Library

Print ISBN: 978 1 84908 431 4
ePDF: 978 1 84908 432 1
ePub: 978 1 84908 834 3

Page layout by Mark Holt
Battlescene artwork by Howard Gerrard
Index by Alison Worthington
Typeset in Sabon and Univers
Originated by PDQ Media
Printed and bound in India by Replika Press Private Ltd.

MIX
Paper from
responsible sources
FSC® C016779

23 24 25 26 27   15 14 13 12 11 10 9

Dedication
In memory of my brother Earl Thompson (1931–2010).
He was a "Steely-Eyed Missile Man" who helped get the Apollo 13
astronauts home.

Acknowledgments
The author would like to thank the following individuals who lent
encouragement and assistance in preparing this book:
Joe Davis, Steve Dick, Ron Flook, Jeff Knox, Tom Knox, Pete and Prue
Mason, T.J. Mullin, Robert Wilkinson-Latham; and three who are no
longer with us: Rex Applegate, Dorothea Fairbairn, and Kelly Yeaton.

The Woodland Trust
Osprey Publishing supports the Woodland Trust, the UK's leading
woodland conservation charity.

www.ospreypublishing.com
To find out more about our authors and books visit our website.
Here you will find extracts, author interviews, details of forthcoming
events and the option to sign-up for our newsletter.

Conversions
The measurements in this book are provided in imperial only. The
following will help in converting between metric and imperial:
- 1 mile = 1.6km
- 1lb = 0.45kg
- 1 yard = 0.9m
- 1ft = 0.3m
- 1in = 25.4mm

Glossary

CHAPE	metal tip of a scabbard or sheath
CROSSGUARD	the protruding bars between blade and hilt
DROP FORGED	a process used to shape metal into complex shapes by dropping heated metal into a punch and die, which is then compressed
HOLLOW GROUND	a knife blade which has been ground to create a characteristic concave, beveled cutting edge. It yields a very sharp but weak edge which requires stropping for maintenance
KNURLED/KNURLING	a diamond-shaped pattern cut into hilts
PALM SWELL	a hilt shaped to fit the palm
POMMEL	the counterweight at the end of the hilt
QUILLON	another term for crossguard
RICASSO	the flat portion on the blade of a dagger just in front of the crossguard
SKULL CRUSHER	a type of pommel designed to allow a dagger to be reversed and used as a bludgeon
TANG	the section of a knife's blade that extends under the hilt

Imperial War Museum Collections
Many of the photos in this book come from the Imperial War
Museum's huge collections which cover all aspects of conflict
involving Britain and the Commonwealth since the start of the
twentieth century. These rich resources are available online to
search, browse and buy at www.iwmcollections.org.uk In addition
to Collections Online, you can visit the Visitor Rooms where you can
explore over 8 million photographs, thousands of hours of moving
images, the largest sound archive of its kind in the world, thousands
of diaries and letters written by people in wartime, and a huge
reference library. To make an appointment, call (020) 7416 5320,
or email: mail@iwm.org.uk
Imperial War Museum www.iwm.org.uk

Image acknowledgments
All images not otherwise credited are from the author's collection.
Cover photographs courtesy IWM (H20410) and author's collection.
Title page image courtesy IWM (H19284).

CONTENTS

INTRODUCTION

Many fighting blades have achieved iconic status over the centuries. The Roman *gladius*, the Scottish claymore, the Saracen scimitar, and the American Bowie – all resonate in the imagination, and each is forever associated with the fighting men who used it. Among more recent blades, none has achieved such an iconic status as the Fairbairn-Sykes (F-S) dagger. Created for the new Commando force during World War II, using experience learned from Shanghai knife-fighting experiments of the 1930s, the "Commando dagger" was the fighting knife of this new breed of soldier, and for half a century it has remained the symbol of military elites around the world.

The F-S dagger was designed for the World War II British Commandos, arguably the forerunners of every modern special forces unit from the Rangers to the SAS. In June 1940, when the Commandos were formed to take the war to the Germans, Britain found itself in a tenuous position – driven out of Europe and fearing German invasion. Firearms were in short supply, to the extent that early Commandos drew their Thompson submachine guns when leaving for a raid and turned them in upon their return so that another Commando unit could use them – woe to any man who lost his! Appeals even had to be made to Canadian and US sport shooters to donate weapons to arm the British Home Guard. The issuing of a handgun to each Commando as a secondary weapon, a common practice among special forces units today, was not an option.

Additionally, those behind the project wanted to instill aggressiveness in the Commandos, an aggressiveness which would let them close with the enemy and help him die for the Reich using cold steel. What the instigators of the Commando project wanted to see was the same spirit of attack with the blade that had allowed Highlanders to rout Indian Mutineers at the point of the bayonet, and that had often caused an enemy to surrender rather than face Gurkhas and their kukris.

A fearsome-looking dagger ideal for silent killing, the Fairbairn-Sykes was both an effective close combat weapon and a symbol of the Commandos' deadliness and elite status. Indeed, the Commando dagger would become a symbol not just to the men who were issued it, but also to British civilians at a time when Britain was on the back foot, and any deadly new way to strike back at the Germans was a boost for morale. Of course, British and American bombers would do that too – from 15,000ft – but the F-S dagger was a potent emblem of Britain's readiness to fight ruthlessly, hand-to-hand with cold steel. Patriotic posters, magazines, novels, movies – all used the Commando dagger as a symbol of the British fighting spirit.

The reputation of its designers has also helped to make the F-S dagger such an iconic weapon. William Ewart Fairbairn and Eric Anthony Sykes are considered among the most important pioneers in modern close combat techniques, whether with bare hands, with clubs, with firearms, or with the blade; naturally, the dagger that bears their name also shares some of their cachet. Some collectors believe that Fairbairn and/or Sykes inspected each 1st Pattern Fairbairn-Sykes dagger; hence, by owning one the collector touches the same steel that was held by these legendary fighters. The story is of doubtful veracity, but it remains a strong image.

One tactic which the Commandos practiced with their Fairbairn-Sykes daggers was silent elimination of sentries. The carotid thrust as illustrated by these Commandos going through training at Achnacarry was a standard move. Note the "victim" also carries his F-S dagger. (Imperial War Museum H26613)

Today, the F-S dagger offers fertile ground for collectors as there are myriad variations, and at least a few have the name of a former owner etched on the blade, offering the chance to research his military career. Although the earliest and rarest Commando daggers now command relatively high prices, interesting 2nd and 3rd Pattern daggers may still be found at a fair cost. And bargains do turn up at flea markets, yard sales, and elsewhere.

Though it was designed 70 years ago, the Fairbairn-Sykes dagger is still a part of many special forces units. In recent years, Wilkinson and other makers have sold many daggers to military units for use as presentation pieces, as some units award an F-S-type dagger to graduates from airborne, special forces, Ranger, or other elite training programs. Other units still issue a version of the F-S as their standard fighting knife. Some custom knife makers offer finely crafted versions of the Commando dagger – sometimes with Damascus blades and handles of exotic materials.

The F-S dagger has charisma, a charisma which can be felt by anyone who holds one and feels the balance. There is a certain warrior spirit in the F-S that seems to flow into the hands of those who handle it. Those same aspects of the Commando dagger that resonated in 1940 still do so today. That's why the Fairbairn-Sykes fighting knife is such a classic.

Two Wilkinson-made 2nd Pattern F-S daggers, one with an all-bright finish and the other with an all-blackened finish; less reflective blackened ones were more desirable in combat.

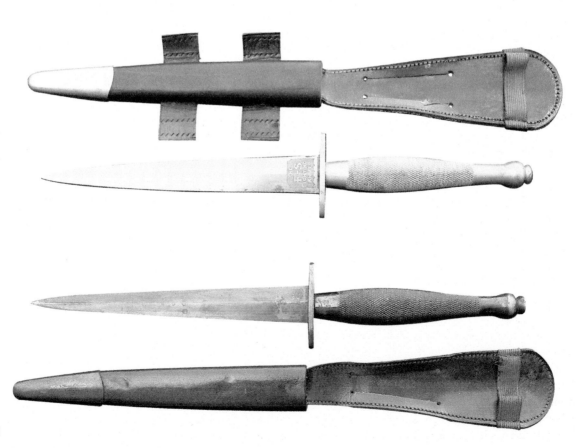

DEVELOPMENT
A fighting knife for the Commandos

SHANGHAI BEGINNINGS

Shanghai during the years between World War I and World War II was the commercial hub of China. Banking, commerce, import/export, and industry were the reason for Shanghai's existence. In fact, what became the Shanghai International Settlement had been established in the mid-19th century to serve British commercial interests, though the American concession was merged with the British one in 1863, thus creating the International Settlement. Eventually, citizens of other countries which had extraterritoriality (the right to be tried only in their own countries' courts) established themselves in the International Settlement as well. After the Sino-Japanese War of 1894–95, Japan gained the same rights as other nations, and they would eventually become a power in the International Settlement. The French had their own concession which bordered the International Settlement, as did the Greater Shanghai area which was under Chinese control. Due to continued unrest throughout China, Chinese businessmen and workers also flocked to Shanghai, where the more stable government and economy of the International Settlement and French concession offered a better standard of living.

By 1934, Shanghai was the sixth largest city in the world. As the Communist Party and the Nationalist Party grew in power in China, conflict was common between warlords across the country, and violence spilled over into Shanghai. Armed robberies and kidnappings became endemic, especially when soldiers from defeated warlord armies entered this rich and divided international city. In 1927, for example, there were 123 murders and 1,458 armed robberies in the International Settlement alone. Political murders and labor unrest, often fueled by Communist agitators, made conditions even more dangerous in Shanghai during the 1920s and 1930s. After 1932 and especially after 1937, Japanese influence and violence (aggravated by Japanese-allied criminals) created still more problems. Organized crime, particularly involving the Green Gang, the principal criminal gang in Shanghai, added potency to this dangerous mix. Drugs, prostitution, gambling, counterfeiting, murder-for-hire – all of the typical crimes associated with "gangsterism" were in Shanghai in abundance. Sometimes called "the most sinful city in the world" and at other times "the most dangerous city in the world," Shanghai usually lived up to its reputation.

However, in the International Settlement, the Shanghai Municipal Police (SMP) offered a counterforce to crime. Generally considered among the best trained and most advanced in the world, the very active SMP Special Branch constantly monitored the currents of crime and politics that surged around the International Settlement, while the regular SMP, trained to high standards of armed and unarmed combat, attempted to keep the streets safe. The police themselves represented the diverse nature of Shanghai. Large numbers of Chinese served as constables, with a few reaching higher rank, while Sikhs and White Russians who had fled to Shanghai after the Russian Revolution were also constables, with many White Russians becoming sergeants. A substantial number of Japanese also served, especially in Hongkew and other areas with large Japanese populations. Higher ranks were filled primarily by "foreign" officers, mostly British.

Many veterans of the Shanghai Municipal Police would return to the UK or the USA to teach the lessons in surviving deadly encounters that they had learned on the streets of Shanghai. Fairbairn and Sykes were just the most famous of these SMP veterans.

Rising from sergeant major/drill instructor in 1917 to assistant commissioner in 1935, the rank at which he retired in 1940, William Ewart Fairbairn trained the men of the SMP in close combat. He had studied deadly Shanghai encounters first-hand while developing the close combat doctrine for SMP firearms training. Having studied at the famous Kodokan judo school in Tokyo, Fairbairn had been one of the first Westerners to achieve black belt rank in jiujitsu. He also studied other martial arts in the process of developing his own style of fighting, which would later be known as Defendu. His techniques were the basis for SMP close combat training without firearms.

Fairbairn had also formed the SMP Reserve Unit, which had a mission similar to a modern Special Weapons and Tactics (SWAT) team – responding to armed encounters, barricaded suspects, kidnapping/hostage incidents, and other serious crimes. Fairbairn's friend Eric Anthony Sykes held a "Specials" commission with the SMP Reserve Unit, where he commanded the snipers. Not only did Fairbairn gain even more experience in tactical firearms usage and street combat with the Reserve Unit, but his position also him gave supervision over the SMP armory where he had access to skilled craftsmen who could implement some of his ideas (e.g. blocking the safeties on the Colt automatic pistols used by SMP personnel, so that they would not forget to release the safety when they had to draw and engage an armed attacker quickly). Fairbairn's books

Defendu (1926) and *Scientific Self Defense* (1931) helped disseminate his style of hand-to-hand combat around the world. One of those who had read Fairbairn's works and practiced the techniques they contained was Sam Yeaton, a young US Marine officer. Assigned to the 4th Marines in Shanghai in 1932, one of Yeaton's top priorities was to contact Fairbairn. Soon Sam Yeaton, as well his two friends, Sam Moore and Sam Taxis, were training with Fairbairn and sharing knowledge of martial arts techniques. From these training sessions ensued discussions about knives for close combat and the most effective techniques to use them and to counter them.

Using the resources of the SMP armory, Fairbairn had some prototype knives made to fit the requirements developed by the "three Sams" and himself. The design was intended as a close combat knife which would allow its wielder to inflict serious injury quickly to stop a fight. The original specifications developed by the group called for a 7in blade with a taper to allow fast in-and-out cuts, a hilt with a palm swell to allow a sure grip when thrusting and pulling the blade back out for follow-up slashes or thrusts, and a hilt-heavy balance. The prototypes made at the SMP armory reportedly used blades from 1888 Lee Metford or 1903 Enfield bayonets

The staff of the Shanghai Municipal Police Armory where early forerunners of the F-S dagger were fabricated; Eric Sykes is second from the left, second row, and William Fairbairn is third from the left next to Sykes. (Dorothea Fairbairn)

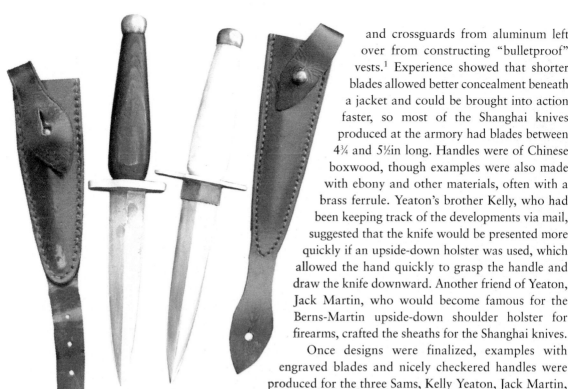

and crossguards from aluminum left over from constructing "bulletproof" vests.[1] Experience showed that shorter blades allowed better concealment beneath a jacket and could be brought into action faster, so most of the Shanghai knives produced at the armory had blades between 4¾ and 5½in long. Handles were of Chinese boxwood, though examples were also made with ebony and other materials, often with a brass ferrule. Yeaton's brother Kelly, who had been keeping track of the developments via mail, suggested that the knife would be presented more quickly if an upside-down holster was used, which allowed the hand quickly to grasp the handle and draw the knife downward. Another friend of Yeaton, Jack Martin, who would become famous for the Berns-Martin upside-down shoulder holster for firearms, crafted the sheaths for the Shanghai knives.

Once designs were finalized, examples with engraved blades and nicely checkered handles were produced for the three Sams, Kelly Yeaton, Jack Martin, and Fairbairn. Fairbairn's was a gift from the Marines. According to W.L. Cassidy, an authority on Fairbairn, the Fairbairn family referred to the Shanghai dagger presented to Fairbairn as the "Mexican Knife." At least one of this type was made for Fairbairn, and he often carried it. Other plain examples were produced in the armory for friends of Fairbairn or the Marines, and possibly also for some of the craftsmen in the armory. Estimates for the number of these knives produced are usually between ten and 20. However, the author has been told that at least a few daggers with the Shanghai characteristics were made during World War II by Alcock & Pierce in Australia and/or Bruce Hand who had worked for Alcock & Pierce. Since some of the Russians who had worked in the SMP armory ended up in Australia there could be a connection – or not!

Fairbairn retired from the SMP in 1940 and returned to England, as did Sykes. Sykes's contacts within the intelligence services helped them gain commissions to train special forces and agents. Sam Yeaton and the other US Marine officers who had practiced martial arts and exchanged ideas on close combat with Fairbairn went on to other postings. Sam Yeaton would go on to command the 3rd Marine Raider Battalion during World War II, whose Marine Raider stiletto knives would also be influenced by the fighting knives that Fairbairn and Sykes developed, and hence by the SMP's experiences in Shanghai.

Forerunners of the F-S dagger, fabricated in the Shanghai Municipal Police Armory to the specifications of William Fairbairn, Sam Yeaton, Sam Moore and Sam Taxis.

[1] Robert Wilkinson-Latham, the grandson of John Wilkinson-Latham who worked with Fairbairn and Sykes on the design of the dagger, has expressed doubts based on the design of the Lee-Metford that it (or indeed any bayonet) would have been used. However, letters sent from Sam Yeaton to his brother Kelly when the knives were being fabricated indicated that bayonets were used.

The engraved Shanghai dagger presented to Fairbairn by US Marines involved in its development. The shoulder sheath system was developed by Jack Martin, later famous for the Berns-Martin "Lightning" shoulder holster for handguns. (Dorothea Fairbairn)

WORLD WAR II: ARMING THE COMMANDOS

Having returned to wartime Europe, Fairbairn and Sykes were commissioned as captains and assigned to train the newly formed Commandos as well as Special Operations Executive (SOE). Formed as part of Winston Churchill's plan to "set Europe ablaze," the Commandos and SOE were intended to keep the spirit of attack alive among British forces by carrying out raids or committing acts of sabotage. Later, when the Allies were ready for large-scale operations, the Commandos would spearhead the conventional attack while SOE would carry out sabotage to hinder the Germans. The deadly skills gained on the streets of Shanghai – especially methods for quickly and silently eliminating an adversary – were incorporated into the training programs for these units.

Early instructors at the Commando Training Centre at Achnacarry, Scotland, were teaching techniques for the use of the blade, but at this point the Commandos had adopted no special knife for the purpose; reportedly, a limited number of Wilkinson RBD hunting knives or "784" double-edged knives were obtained for instructional use. The RBD knife took its name from R. Beauchamp Drummond, the Scottish outdoorsman who had originally had Wilkinson produce an example to his specifications. At least some World War I-era Robbins Dudley knives were used, as was the BC41 knuckle knife. In limited numbers, other knives also appear to have been used by the Commandos during their early days as the Independent Companies.

Many aspects of the earliest involvement of Wilkinson Sword remain vague. Knives exist which were allegedly for Commando use and fabricated from surplus 1903 Enfield or 1888 Lee-Metford bayonets. These early daggers show some characteristics that would later be associated with the Fairbairn-Sykes dagger. Their 7½in blades were of double-edged, tapered, needlepoint type. Hilts were checkered and of "coke-bottle" configuration. Some early hilts were of steel, while others were of brass. The crossguards were straight, and some examples had a cutout to allow the thumb to be

Fighting the Fairbairn-Sykes Way

William Fairbairn's career was devoted to perfecting the techniques of fighting, whether with knives, pistols, or bare hands. After joining the Royal Marines in 1901, he later served in the Legation Guard in Korea where he began studying various martial arts techniques, including sport bayonet fighting. In December 1907, Fairbairn left the Royal Marines and joined the Shanghai Municipal Police as a constable and by 1917 he had risen to the rank of sergeant major/drill instructor. Although Fairbairn appears to have had an interest in martial skills during his service in Korea, it was reportedly an incident in Shanghai, when he was severely beaten while on patrol, that inspired him to begin a serious study of Asian martial arts. However, Fairbairn was willing to learn from anyone who had something to teach. The presence in Shanghai of practitioners of Chinese, Japanese, French, English, and Indian martial arts among others allowed Fairbairn to learn from a variety of sources, though jiujitsu was his primary discipline. He later trained in judo with a Japanese inspector from the SMP and in kung fu with a Chinese master.

From these disciplines, Fairbairn developed a system that was designed to enable members of the SMP to prevail in violent encounters on the streets of Shanghai, and in 1915, these techniques formed the basis for the *Shanghai Municipal Police Manual of Self-Defense*. Other police departments around the world would adopt many of Fairbairn's precepts in training their own officers. As Fairbairn's own experience increased, he created what today would be called a police defense tactics system, which he termed "Defendu." He published a manual of Defendu in 1926, but his later book expanding on the techniques, *Scientific Self Defense*, is much better known. Defendu is still studied today by many practitioners.

To give the officers more survivability in gun battles, Fairbairn developed techniques of close combat with the automatic pistol and arranged for foreign officers to be armed with the Colt 1911A1 and Chinese officers with the Colt Pocket Model 1908. Fairbairn's firearms training focused on teaching officers realistic engagement skills that would carry over onto the streets. The safeties of the pistols were pinned and officers were taught to draw and pull the slide back to chamber a round as they prepared to engage. They went into a crouch and, using instinctive point shooting, fired two shots at the chest of an assailant.

Fairbairn was a great believer in realistic training and developed an obstacle course over which trainees had to run prior to engaging

BELOW 1940: British SOE operatives train in the pistol-shooting methods Fairbairn and Sykes honed on the streets of Shanghai a decade previously. (IWM H5461)

targets on the range; this simulated the need to fight after chasing a suspect through the streets and over the rooftops of Shanghai. He also developed "houses of horror" through which a trainee would pass and have to engage targets when he encountered them. Another Fairbairn innovation was the use of ammunition with bullets bearing the letters "SMP" so that it could be proved whether someone had or had not been shot by a member of the force – as there were always claims after a gunfight that the police had shot innocent bystanders.

After an incident in which a group of protesting students was fired upon, in 1926, Fairbairn formed the SMP Reserve Unit, the predecessor of modern SWAT teams. Members of the Reserve Unit were skilled at riot control, hostage rescue, dealing with barricaded suspects, raids on dangerous opium dens, and escort of dangerous prisoners or transfers of large sums of cash. Many tactics still used by SWAT teams and special operations units on raids were developed initially in Shanghai. The Reserve Unit also pioneered the use of snipers to quickly eliminate a criminal. Fairbairn's friend Eric Sykes led a group of skilled long-range, competition rifle shooters – all of whom were part-time officers, or "specials" – who formed the sniper unit. In another pioneering move for the SMP, members of the Reserve Unit were armed with the Thompson submachine gun – anticipating the later common use of automatic weapons for police tactical operations.

Many of those who knew Fairbairn and Sykes feel that Sykes was actually the more knowledgeable about firearms. He had been an avid shooter for years and represented Colt, Remington, Kynoch, and many other arms manufacturers in China. He had also competed at Bisley and in matches throughout China. Fairbairn, on the other hand, was the more knowledgeable about hand-to-hand, stick, and knife combat. Over the years of working together, each learned much of the other's expertise. Although Sykes carried out his function as an arms representative and also sold real estate, it is now accepted that he was also an agent of MI6. This helped Fairbairn and Sykes gain commissions in the British Army and to be assigned to train SOE, the Commandos, and, in Fairbairn's case, the OSS.

Fairbairn and Sykes brought their knowledge of close combat to the training of Commandos and agents. Other members of the SMP who had trained with Fairbairn, such as Pat O'Neill who trained the 1st Special Service Force, spread the tenets of Shanghai close combat even further, as did other instructors who took what they had learned from Fairbairn or Sykes back to their units. Fairbairn was assigned to the OSS training facility in Canada during 1942, while Sykes remained in the UK to train SOE operatives. Their 1942 book, *Shooting to Live*, was widely used as a text during World War II. Sykes, whose real name was Eric Anthony Schwabe (he had changed it because of anti-German

ABOVE William Ewart Fairbairn was involved in the development of the dagger which bears his name, and in training the Commandos and others in its use. Here he is photographed in the uniform of an assistant commissioner of the Shanghai Municipal Police. (Dorothea Fairbairn)

feeling during World War I), died in 1945. Fairbairn, however, continued his work with OSS and later with the military government in Germany, rising to the rank of lieutenant-colonel by the end of the war.

In the postwar years, Fairbairn continued to refine his techniques and carried out training for units such as the Singapore Police and Cyprus Police, the latter in 1956 when he was 71. Reportedly, he was still capable of throwing policemen half his age around with little trouble. The combat techniques developed by Fairbairn and Sykes, as well as their training methods, are still used today by military special operations units and police forces around the world. They are simple and practical and easily applied on the streets or battlefield. That is what has given the Shanghai techniques such currency, 70 years after the International Settlement ceased to exist.

An early "WSC" Fairbairn-Sykes-type dagger fabricated from a bayonet; although some dispute that these are forerunners to the F-S dagger, Fairbairn himself stated there were a few hundred produced from bayonets prior to production of the 1st Pattern F-S. Note that this dagger has the 3in S-guard. The sheath is of a type known as "Camp X sheaths" designed to button inside the trousers for concealment.

placed for a "fencing grip," in which the blade protrudes from the front of the hand as with a sword. The scabbards for at least some of these early knives are easily identifiable as they were produced by cutting up "leg of mutton" shotgun cases and, therefore, have green baize linings.

It is debatable whether Wilkinson had anything to do with these blades; Robert Wilkinson-Latham does not feel that they did, though some collectors consider them to be examples of pre-Fairbairn-Sykes daggers. Fairbairn himself wrote that Wilkinson made the first few hundred F-S-type knives from old bayonets, at his behest. According to the special forces writer Peter Mason, early in World War II Fairbairn once came into his father's pub with one of these "pre-F-S" daggers fabricated from a bayonet.

Around this time, one other cutler, John Paisley of Glasgow, was reportedly also making early Commando daggers of similar type, some with brass hilts and others with hardwood hilts. One of the most interesting variations made by Paisley was the "suicide" dagger supposedly designed for members of X Troop of 10 Commando. X Troop, comprised of German-speakers, was assigned many missions behind German lines where their language skills allowed them to move more freely. However, they were likely to be tortured if captured by the Germans, especially since many were Jews who had fled Germany; hence, at least some ordered a dagger with a tang that did not go all the way through the handle, so that a small compartment could be incorporated to carry a suicide capsule. To facilitate getting the capsule quickly, often a small spring was incorporated that would pop it out as the "pommel nut" which hid the chamber was removed. In other examples the checkered hilt was actually cut and threaded so that by twisting it separated to reveal the capsule compartment. Only a small number of the "suicide" daggers were ever made since it was realized that captured Commandos would have their knives taken away immediately, and thus they might not be able to reach the capsule. Instead, the capsules were usually hidden about the clothing. Once again, little is known about these early Commando knives, and collectors disagree as to whether they should really be considered as prototypes of the F-S.

In November 1940, Fairbairn and Sykes met with the director of Wilkinson Sword, John Wilkinson-Latham, to discuss a knife designed for the Commandos. Although Fairbairn had taken along one of his Shanghai knives, many of the features that would be incorporated into what would become known as the Fairbairn-Sykes dagger were actually drawn from previous Wilkinson designs. During the discussions, Fairbairn emphasized the importance of the knife being hilt-heavy, and according to some reports used a ruler to demonstrate on Sykes the use of a double-edged blade for thrusting deep in silent killing. In fact, Fairbairn was reportedly not happy that the resulting Fairbairn-Sykes blade did not resemble the Shanghai knife more closely. There are aspects of both the Shanghai daggers and the pre-F-S Wilkinson design in what would become the F-S dagger eventually acquired by the Commandos. Robert Wilkinson-

Latham also points out that there are strong indications that his grandfather John Wilkinson-Latham incorporated features from a knife that Wilkinson had made in 1931 for a gentleman named Lynch. The double-edged blade and distinctive ricasso – the flat portion on the blade just in front of the crossguard – of the Lynch dagger certainly resemble those of the F-S.

As the specifications for the Commando dagger emerged, this new knife was to have a heavy checkered hilt, a double-edged blade and a crossguard to protect the knuckles and thumb. Note that the term "stiletto," which is often used to describe the Fairbairn-Sykes dagger, is not strictly speaking correct. The F-S was designed for both thrusting and slashing, while stilettos were normally intended for thrusting. That said, in some instances in this book, the term "stiletto" may be used to describe the F-S just because it has achieved common usage.

Once the specifications were agreed, Wilkinson-Latham met with Charles Ross, the head of Wilkinson's experimental workshop, to discuss their requirements for the dagger, which would be passed to the Wilkinson grinding foreman so that a prototype could be produced. This prototype was then shown to those involved in the design, and, once approved, was

In 1941, members of 3 Commando receive some of the earliest F-S daggers produced. (IWM H20427)

used to create the tooling for production F-S knives. Since the War Office desperately needed blades to train the Commandos, it was at this point that the Wilkinson RBD and "784" knives mentioned previously were ordered.

Based upon prototypes supplied, orders were placed for somewhere between 6,000 and 7,500 of the Wilkinson F-S dagger. SOE and the other "special forces" units would also order somewhere near 1,000 within a short time. Capt Leslie Wood, Royal Engineers, was the representative who ordered these knives for various units. The agreed price was 13 shillings, 6 pence (13s 6d) – equivalent to about £30 in 2010 value or, based on an exchange rate to sterling in 1940 of $4.25, to $127.50 in today's dollars. Wood played an important role in the development and, especially, the acquisition of the F-S dagger as he was in charge of procurement for SOE, the Commandos, and other special units. Wood may also have played a part in recruiting Fairbairn and Sykes to train SOE and the Commandos.

A Commando examines the blade of his 1st Pattern F-S dagger. (IWM H20416)

Another knife which has intrigued collectors, but whose origins are hazy, is very similar to the 1st Pattern F-S, having the flat ricasso, double-edged spear-point blade, 3in S-curved crossguard (some refer to these as "recurved quillions"), and brass coke-bottle hilt. But instead of the etched Wilkinson and F-S logos which would appear on what is often known as the "1st Pattern" F-S, this dagger just had the initials "WSC" stamped into the ricasso. The author has heard figures for the number produced of between 100 and 500, but has not been able to confirm a total. This knife is extremely rare, reportedly because a fire caused by an air raid resulted in the destruction of most of the knives before they could be issued for field testing, and it is questionable if any were ever issued. Of the few examples the author has seen, many have shown fire damage which seems to give some validity to this story. As there is no mention of these knives in Wilkinson records, Robert Wilkinson-Latham does not consider them to have been Wilkinson preproduction knives, although those examined by the author show high quality in manufacture. Since this knife is very similar to what would become the first production knives for the Commandos, some speculate that they were produced before the transfer for the etched ricasso markings became available.

THE PRODUCTION F-S DAGGERS

The 1st Pattern F-S dagger

The first production F-S dagger which would be issued to the Commandos, SOE, and others had a 6⅞in double-edged blade with a flat ricasso; as a knife-fighting expert, Fairbairn among others believed that a fighting knife should have a blade at least 6in long to allow penetration of an enemy's vitals even through heavy clothing. On one side of the ricasso was etched "F-S Fighting Knife" and on the other a Wilkinson Sword logo, and these handmade blades were drop forged. Examination of a substantial number of these early F-S daggers reveals two slightly different blade types: one with a slimmer "stiletto" blade and another with a wider, more spear-point blade. These differences are minor and are no doubt because each blade was individually ground.

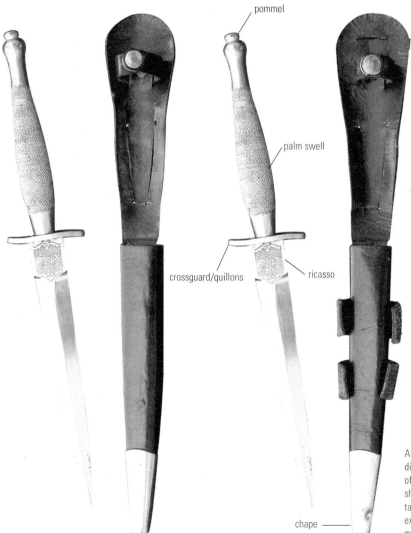

pommel

palm swell

crossguard/quillons

ricasso

chape

A pair of 1st Pattern F-S daggers displaying the logo on each side of the ricasso; note that the sheath on the right retains the tabs, but like some other early examples, the one on the left was manufactured without tabs.

The crossguard was S-shaped; originally it was 3in long but it was soon changed for 2in ones as the 3in crossguards tended to snag on clothing, ropes, etc. Some view the 3in S-guard as a separate knife produced before the 2in S-guard, but those who consider the "WSC" knife to be a preproduction 1st Pattern F-S believe that the remaining 3in S-guards made for the WSC knives were just being used up on the first production 1st Patterns. This may, indeed, mean that those F-S daggers with the 3in guard are the earliest, but it is not certain. The grip on the 1st Pattern F-S was checkered brass with the palm swell often called the "coke-bottle" grip. The blade's tang passed through the crossguard and hilt and a threaded nut was tightened down to hold the assembled knife together. Any portion of the tang still protruding was ground off and then hammered flat with the top of the pommel nut.

Sheaths for the 1st Pattern F-S had a belt loop and two sets of tabs, which would allow the sheath to be sewn to the battledress. Although this was a convenient system, most early F-S knives have the tabs cut off. The author has been told by former Commandos that the first time it was necessary to wash their clothing they took a razor blade and cut the sheath free, then just used the belt loops in the future. Most early users ignored the tabs and did not sew them to clothing. According to Robert Wilkinson-Latham, some very early sheaths were produced without the tabs. A snap retention strap was included to keep the dagger in the sheath. The chape was nickeled, though some Commandos dulled it with shoe polish for operations. There was no locket at the mouth of the sheath and the crossguard of the F-S rested on the leather. Since a price of 4s 6d is given in Wilkinson records for the sheaths (many of which were in fact outsourced) it may be assumed that they were charged for separately. The author has been told that the earliest sheaths were fabricated by Parker of St Martin's Lane. Reportedly, Curtis Lloyds in Lewes, Sussex, and Larkin in Eastbourne, Sussex, later made sheaths for Commando daggers as well.

Close-up of markings on the ricasso of 1st Pattern F-S daggers.

Some of the earliest 1st Pattern F-S knives made in late 1940 were fabricated mostly by hand. To increase production, however, by January 1941, more machine work was being carried out. There were four basic parts to the 1st Pattern F-S and later versions – the drop-forged blade, stamped crossguard, brass grip (which was turned and bored on a lathe) and brass top nut. It can be assumed that on 1st Pattern knives, the crossguard was bent by hand. Handles were hand checkered, while blades were hand ground by Jack Mappin, who had been working for Wilkinson for over 20 years. After sharpening, blades were polished and the tang was threaded. Next, the logos were etched onto the ricasso. Crossguards, handles, pommel nuts, and sheath chapes were polished then heavily nickeled. Finally, knives and sheaths were hand assembled and inspected.

Once the early knives were in production, some were shipped to Commando supply depots, but many Commandos picked theirs up at Wilkinson's showroom by presenting a requisition for them. Some chose to have their names engraved; however, since Wilkinson was working at full capacity to produce the necessary knives, it is unlikely many would have been named. Hence, a 1st Pattern F-S with owner's name engraved is an especially interesting piece. SOE orders were also picked up or delivered to SOE training schools.

Among F-S collectors there has been a continuing discussion about how many of the 1st Pattern F-S were produced before they were replaced by the 2nd Pattern knife in August 1941. Some researchers have stated a production of around 1,250, but Robert Wilkinson-Latham offers information from Wilkinson records which indicates that as many as 7,000 1st Pattern F-S daggers may have been produced. Based on the numbers of this dagger that the author has personally examined over the last 40 years, he believes that production is well into the thousands as the Wilkinson records suggest. The author has seen figures that 350,000 F-S knives were produced from all sources before 1945, but this figure may actually be very low (see below). Certainly, the production of the 1st Pattern was quite small by comparison.

Simplifying the design: the 2nd Pattern

An order from now Maj Wood in August 1941 specified that F-S daggers should be of the "new design." This new design was a simplified version of the F-S to allow Wilkinson to produce the knife more quickly and without the need for the hand finishing required for the 1st Pattern. It allowed workers with less experience to carry out some operations and also eased quality control. (It is important to remember that Wilkinson had other military contracts and hence could not devote too many resources to the F-S knives.)

One of the greatest time-savers was extending the diamond-shaped blade all the way to the tang, thus eliminating the flat ricasso. Though this ricasso gave the 1st Pattern a very distinctive look, it was quite labor-intensive to produce and really offered no advantage, though it may have been originally intended to offer a better blade-catching design for knife-to-knife combat. Some Commandos and airborne troops liked the new full-length double edge as they felt it gave a longer cutting surface for use on ropes, parachute lines, etc. Other timesaving changes included replacing the S-guard with a straight crossguard and casting the grip rather than turning it. The Wilkinson logo and F-S Fighting Knife logo were retained, though the transfer for the etching was enlarged to look more proportional on the diamond blade. Predictably, during the early months of the production of what would become known as the 2nd Pattern F-S, some remaining parts from the 1st Pattern knife may have been used.

The SAS in North Africa (previous pages)

The F-S dagger was in action within months of its introduction. Here, during a December 1941 raid against an Afrika Korps airfield, one member of the Special Air Service (SAS) silently eliminates a German sentry with a carotid thrust with his 1st Pattern dagger, while the other SAS member places a Lewes bomb on a Luftwaffe fuel truck. The 6$^7/_8$in blade of the 1st Pattern was designed to penetrate through to a vital organ or artery even through heavy clothing, such as the greatcoats often worn by the Germans.

In December, 1941, Maj Wood placed the last order from his office for 1,000 2nd Pattern F-S daggers. Reportedly, many of these were to be supplied to the Auxiliary Units, which were designed as "stay behind" guerilla forces should the UK be invaded. Interestingly, among officers assigned to forming and training the Auxiliary Units was Capt Peter Fleming of the Grenadier Guards, Ian Fleming's brother.

Once this order was fulfilled, Wilkinson did not receive any major official orders for some time. There was an order for 120 F-S daggers from the Latvian government-in-exile, however, and quite a few daggers were supplied to individual purchasers at Wilkinson's Pall Mall shop. Some of these personal purchase daggers showed special finishes – often all black or black with a bright blade – as well as etched banners with names or initials on the blade. Wilkinson charged 1s 6d for this personalized etching. The author has seen many private purchase F-S daggers with etched banners for members of the US Air Corps, who began arriving in the UK in substantial numbers during 1942.

A member of 3 Commando with a 2nd Pattern F-S between his teeth during training at Achnacarry; although this looks quite "aggressive," it was really only practical in specific tactical situations (e.g. climbing over the side of a ship or a wall when both hands were needed, yet when a sentry might have to be instantly eliminated). (IWM H19284)

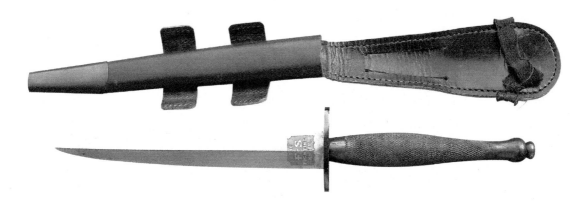

A nice example of a 2nd Pattern F-S made by Wilkinson and retaining the "F-S Fighting Knife" logo; note that the flat ricasso has been eliminated to speed production. (Jeff Knox)

In October 1942, the design of the 2nd Pattern F-S's sheath was simplified even more when the snap retention strap was eliminated and replaced with an elastic band which slipped over the handle of the F-S to retain it. Many former Commandos and US Army Rangers who used this sheath were not impressed by the modification. The elastic tended to lose its elasticity and stretch or rot from salt spray or perspiration and break. As a result, daggers slipped out and were lost. Many of these sheaths encountered today, if they were actually carried in combat, show deterioration of the elastic retention band. In another labor-saving attempt, the chape for the sheath was flattened so it could be stamped more readily. Around this time, too, the hilt, crossguard, and chape were blackened. This change may have been in response to requests from those using the daggers for night raids.

By the end of 1942, the Ministry of Supply wanted other Sheffield cutlers to start producing F-S daggers of the simplified 2nd Pattern design, and manufacturers included Wostenholm, Rodgers, Clarke, Watts, and BSA (Birmingham Small Arms). Clarke knives are the only ones actually marked with the maker's name. On the crossguard these knives have "J. Clarke & Sons/Sheffield" plus a date and broad arrow. F-S daggers of 2nd Pattern with a B2 mark plus broad arrow are often encountered. Robert Wilkinson-Latham offers good evidence that these were manufactured by BSA; this makes sense, as "B2" knives are relatively common, and BSA reportedly produced a large number of F-S daggers. Examining a substantial number of 2nd Pattern daggers made by Sheffield cutlers reveals a noticeable variation in quality. Some had very crudely checkered grips and the blade quality was substandard on some.

Wilkinson production increased substantially as well. In October 1942 the firm received an order for 38,700 2nd Pattern daggers, followed in February 1943 by an order for 10,000 all-black knives at 17s 6d, though the order was increased the same day by 154,000 more daggers at 17s 4d. This contract remained in effect until the end of the war, and apparently Wilkinson began delivering 3rd Pattern knives to fulfill it once they switched production to that version.

Some 2nd Pattern F-S daggers purchased at Wilkinson's shop were personalized in scrolls on the blade. This one was for an American serving in the Eagle Squadron. (Jeff Knox)

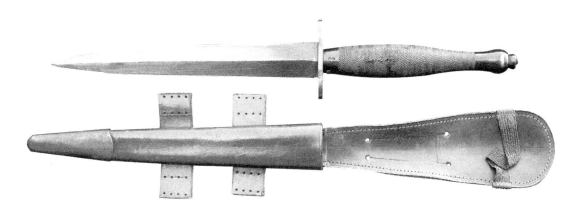

Although 2nd Pattern F-S knives, both from Wilkinson and others, may be found in bright, partial black and partial bright, and all black, the last of these seems to have been most common, which is understandable for a knife intended for combat use as reflection from a bright handle or blade would be more likely to give the user away.

Various cutlers produced 2nd Pattern Commando daggers which lacked the F-S and Wilkinson markings. This one was all black, though some blacking has worn off the blade.

Mass production: the 3rd Pattern

The F-S design was simplified even more for the production of what is generally termed the 3rd Pattern F-S. The most noteworthy change was the switch from hilts of brass, which was a critical war material, to a copper-plated diecast zinc alloy. This grip, which Robert Wilkinson-Latham speculates was designed by Joseph Rodgers, has distinctive ribs rather than checkering. Military knife expert Robert Buerlein has correspondence with the firm indicating that all of the 3rd Pattern grips were cast by Wolverhampton Die Casting Ltd. He advises that they were cast in a four-cavity die which produced four grips at a time. Each cavity was numbered 1–4 for quality control purposes, which explains the numbers found near the pommels on 3rd Pattern grips.

Also eliminated was the flat-ground "V" at the top of the blade which had been incorporated to allow fitting of the crossguard and handle. Since the blades were now machine ground this speeded production even more. Although October 1943 is generally given as the date for the switch to the ribbed handles, each cutler producing the F-S would have used up 2nd Pattern handles still in stock. Wilkinson was still producing 2nd Pattern daggers in late 1943, including some that were blued instead of blackened. An interesting Wilkinson variation sought by collectors uses the 3rd Pattern ribbed grip but still has a blade marked with "F-S Fighting Knife" and the Wilkinson Sword etching.

3rd Pattern Commando dagger showing the cast zinc ribbed handle which simplified production. Note the retention band which shows typical deterioration from combat use and exposure to the elements.

Wilkinson's final order for F-S knives came on February 6, 1943, and ran until it was canceled on April 10, 1945, at which point 163,656 knives had been produced on that final contract. Wilkinson's price on knives for this final contract was 16 shillings, representing the savings in materials and labor on the 3rd Pattern dagger.

Figures quoted by Robert Wilkinson-Latham from the Wilkinson Sword order book indicate that 6,779 1st Pattern, 40,923 2nd Pattern, and 163,565 3rd Pattern were produced for UK government orders. These figures do not include private purchase knives sold at the Pall Mall establishment or some orders from Allied forces. The author has seen figures estimating that a total of 2 million 3rd Pattern Commando daggers may have been produced by Sheffield cutlers during the war. If this is the case, then the 350,000 production figure given earlier may apply to pre-3rd Pattern knives.

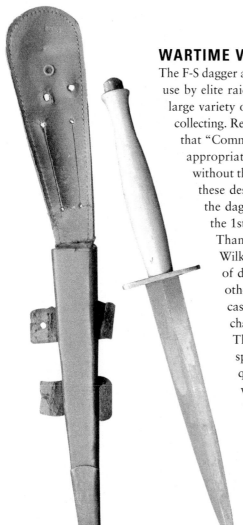

Smooth-handled version of the Commando dagger sometimes attributed to Polish airborne troops.

WARTIME VARIATIONS OF THE F-S DAGGER

The F-S dagger appeals to collectors for various reasons. The cachet of its use by elite raiding forces has certainly added to its mystique, but the large variety of examples available has also made it a fertile field for collecting. Related to this diversity, many collectors and researchers feel that "Commando dagger" or "Commando knife" is actually a more appropriate designation since far more examples were produced without the "F-S" etching than with it. The author feels that any of these designations is valid if discussing the entire production of the daggers, though "F-S dagger" certainly is more correct for the 1st Pattern dagger.

Thanks to Robert Wilkinson-Latham's research in the Wilkinson records, quite a bit is known about the production of daggers by that firm. However, few records exist for the other firms which produced Commando daggers. In most cases, cutlers were working to meet orders and often made changes in materials on the fly if they encountered a shortage. There also seem to have been orders by some units for special versions of the Commando dagger in limited quantities. As a result, collectors may encounter many variations, but little information is available about most of these. The most interesting and/or common of these variations are discussed below.

Many variants differ primarily in their handle material or design. One of the most common is the "ribbed and beaded" (or "ringed and beaded") version; this designation describes the gripping surface of the handle which has both ribs and rings that are patterned to look somewhat like a string of beads. There are differences in the numbers of rows of "beads" on some of these knives, and pommel nuts vary as well. At least some of the "ribbed and beaded" daggers have a broad arrow and one of the numbers 1, 2, 3, 4, or 9 stamped on the base of the grip.[2] It has generally been accepted by researchers and collectors that "ribbed and beaded" daggers were produced for commercial sale; however, these markings seem to indicate that some daggers were produced to a government contract. Some researchers believe that Joseph Rodgers produced the "ribbed and beaded" dagger. A rarely encountered variation has what is termed a "ribbed and roped" handle in which rings that resemble ropes are interspersed with rings. "Ribbed and roped" daggers also have a distinctive acorn-shaped pommel nut. These are very handsome daggers.

Another variation has a gray smooth handle and a crossguard that is more rectangular than the more common oval crossguard. Anecdotally, this dagger has been attributed to Free Polish airborne troops who ordered the daggers while in the UK. However, the standard book on Polish military knives, *Noze Wojska Polskiego*, does not include this knife, showing only standard 2nd and 3rd Pattern knives as having been used by Free Polish forces.

An Australian commando knife was produced, which had a flat ricasso, a wooden or cast handle, and two types of leather scabbard, one of which has a distinctive large metal "eye hole." These knives were produced by Whittingslowe & Gregsteel. Their 7½in blade and 12⅝in overall length makes them obviously larger than a typical F-S.

Free French forces reportedly purchased a Commando dagger which had a slim turned steel handle with a large "button" pommel. The author has also heard that this knife was used by the Maquis (which would be logical if it was made for the Free French). This may be partly based on an example illustrated in Buerlein's *Allied Military Fighting Knives* which bears the inscription "Mort aux Boches"; however, one former member of the SAS, who worked with the Maquis in France, had one of these blades and referred to it in conversation with the author as a "Free French dagger." Photos of Office of Strategic Services (OSS) "Jedburgh" personnel working with Resistance fighters in France also show them carrying this version of the Commando dagger. Some knowledgeable collectors attribute this all-steel version to H.G. Long.

A full-size and a "miniature" dagger of the type generally associated with the Free French forces or the French Resistance.

---

[2] Ron Flook offers sound evidence in his book *British and Commonwealth Military Knives* that these numbers were actually those used by inspectors who may have visited multiple factories; hence, the numbers do not denote a specific manufacturer.

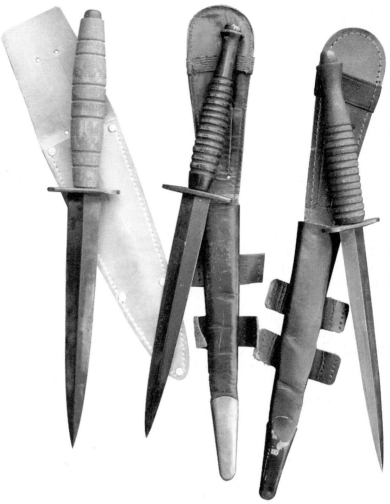

RIGHT
Three examples of Commando daggers produced with wooden handles; note the crude sheath for the example on the left.

BELOW
A Commando dagger reportedly produced during World War II in India or Ceylon; note the sheath's webbed frog.

Commando daggers with ribbed wooden handles are sometimes encountered. Various explanations for these are suggested; applying Occam's Razor, the simplest explanation is that they were made up after one or more cutlers had run out of handles and were using up blades and crossguards – if so, these knives would have been produced late in the war or shortly after it. Another explanation sometimes offered is that these knives were produced in India. The author believes that some wooden-handled Commando daggers were produced in India, as he has one with colored rings on the handle, which was obtained from a former member of the RAF who acquired it in India during the war. In fact, anecdotal evidence does exist for the use of the wooden-handled knives by RAF air crew, not necessarily just in the Far East.

A separate type of "Indian" dagger was produced for issue to Indian troops. These are of 2nd and 3rd Pattern with standard handles and marked with an "I" and broad arrow. Also attributed to Indian airborne troops are William Rodgers Commando daggers, with sheaths fabricated from 1907 bayonet sheaths which retain the frog.

Another Commando dagger made in the Far East – possibly Ceylon, though more likely India – has a purplish blade finish, roughly checkered brass handle, and sheath with a lever in the locket which fits through a slot in the crossguard to act as a retention device. Most of these sheaths have a webbed frog.

An extremely interesting Commando dagger was made, reportedly for 4 Commando, which incorporated a "gigli" wire garrote wrapped around the handle. There were various attempts to produce a combination of dagger and garrote in one weapon, most of which proved less efficient than having the two silent killing weapons separately. The Peskett close combat device, which incorporated a cosh, knife, and garrote was perhaps the most interesting. Generally, combination close combat weapons of this type didn't perform any of their intended functions well.

One of the rarest and most interesting F-S-related items is the leather "arm sheath" or "sleeve scabbard." A small number of these well-made sheaths were reportedly offered for sale as personal purchase items during World War II and used by some paratroopers and members of the SAS, including members of the French and Belgian troops. These sheaths will be discussed in more detail later.

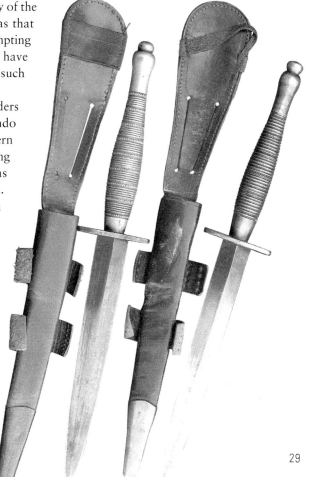

Two examples of the "ribbed and beaded" handle variation seen on some Commando daggers.

The author has also seen an all-black Commando dagger which was reportedly produced in Germany as a copy of the British version during the war. One explanation was that German Abwehr agents used it as a prop when attempting to infiltrate Resistance cells; however, there should have been plenty of captured F-S daggers available for such usage.

Perhaps no variation of the F-S dagger engenders more discussion than the "miniature" Commando dagger or the "agent's" dagger. Miniature 1st Pattern Fairbairn-Sykes daggers certainly exist, but according to Robert Wilkinson-Latham, these were made as window decorations for a 1946 Wilkinson promotion. Collectors who later acquired these developed a myth that they were produced for clandestine issue.

That does not mean that smaller F-S/Commando daggers were not also produced on an individual basis. The author has a couple of such knives, one of which was purchased from a former member of the World War II-era SAS who was later an intelligence officer. He had a "miniature" Commando dagger with a 3rd Pattern handle which was carried in an arm/calf sheath. Miniature Commando daggers have been attributed to H.G. Long, John Paisley, and Alcock & Pierce in Australia. Most have the 3rd Pattern-type handles, though some with brass checkered handles of the 2nd Pattern type have also been noted. (An interesting

Two examples of miniature "agent's" daggers which were generally about ⅔- to ¾-standard size. Small numbers of miniature daggers seem to have been made to individual order. Note that the example at the right, which formerly belonged to a retired British intelligence officer, has an arm or calf sheath.

aside about smaller daggers and other clandestine weapons made by Alcock & Pierce is that Sykes was the Alcock & Pierce agent in Shanghai before the war. He also represented Colt, Remington, Webley & Scott, Kynoch, and Imperial Chemical Industries, among others.) Sheaths are normally of either the arm or calf type with elastic straps or designed to button inside the trousers. Reportedly, the Earl of Suffolk, who was associated with SOE, ordered a group of these compact Commando daggers for presentation to friends in SOE and in other special forces.

In fact, the term "miniature" can be misleading as most of those knives designated as miniature Commando daggers are between 7 and 9in long overall, which puts them between ⅔ and ¾ the overall length of a full-sized F-S dagger. In fact, some collectors refer to these knives as "¾"-size knives. There are also F-S-type daggers which are between the "agent's" dagger and the full-size dagger in size. These are sometimes referred to as "⅞-size" daggers. The assumption has been that these were made to order for smaller individuals.

F-S INFLUENCES: THE AMERICAN FIGHTING KNIVES

The Raider stiletto

The US Marine Raider stiletto owes its design to the F-S dagger. The Marine Raiders were formed in February 1942, and trained to carry out amphibious raiding missions – similar to those of the Commandos – in the Pacific. President Roosevelt was a supporter of the Raiders, in part due to the urging of his son James Roosevelt, a Marine officer who would serve in the 2nd Raider Battalion. Four Raider battalions were authorized, but first a training program had to be developed and men recruited. Marine captains Wallace M. Greene Jr and Samuel B. Griffith Jr were sent to Achnacarry in November 1941 to train with the Commandos and experience their methods. Both men had served with the Marines in China, and in Shanghai Griffith had known Fairbairn; he would later write an article on SMP firearms training. Sam Yeaton, who had worked with Fairbairn on the Shanghai daggers, would eventually command the 3rd Raider Battalion, further cementing the Raider–Fairbairn connection. In 1942, additional Marines were sent through the Commando course to prepare them as Marine Raider instructors. Most who came back were enthusiastic about the F-S dagger.

In order to provide the Raiders with a modern fighting knife, Marine LtCol Clifford Shuey designed a "stiletto" based on the Fairbairn-Sykes dagger. Manufactured by Camillus Cutlery, a total of 15,000 Raider stilettos were reportedly produced, though only 6,000 Marines served as Raiders. Some were used as replacements for stilettos lost or damaged, but it is said that some ended up with the Paramarines, the Corps' airborne troops who would later merge with the Raiders. Some leftover Raider stilettos appear to have been given an all-black finish and then issued to Canadian airborne troops.

The Raider stiletto's blade was double edged and appears similar to the F-S blade. However, it was of substantially thinner stock and was stamped rather than drop forged; hence it was not as strong as the F-S blade. Raider stiletto blades were slightly longer than those of a typical F-S knife, by about ¼in, and were etched with a scroll bearing the letters "USMC." Unlike the handles of F-S daggers, those of the Raider stilettos were made of a zinc alloy and cast directly on to the tang. Sheaths were substantially different from those of the F-S, being fabricated of leather, with both belt loops and a wire bracket to allow attachment to the Marine Corps webbed belt. Sheaths had a hole at the bottom for a leg tie-down to position the sheath and keep it from moving around on the leg. To protect the sheath from the point and edges of the stiletto, staples were affixed to the mouth of the sheath and steel plates were attached at the front and back of the sheath's bottom. According to Robert Buerlein, Raiders discovered they could fit their stiletto sheath behind their .45cal pistol holsters, thus making for a more natural draw of the knife and also keeping it out of the way.

Ironically, when the Raider battalions were disbanded most of the personnel were used to reform the 4th Marines, which had spent so many years peacekeeping in Shanghai – at the time when many of the close combat concepts that would later be used by the Commandos and Raiders were being developed, and where officers of the 4th Marines had helped develop the Shanghai forerunner of the F-S dagger.

The OSS stiletto

The US Office of Strategic Services (OSS) was formed with a mission similar to that of SOE. Many OSS operatives were trained at Camp X in Canada by Fairbairn or Sykes and later Rex Applegate of the OSS itself. As a result, OSS agents were familiar with the F-S dagger and techniques for using it. It is logical, therefore, that when the OSS chose to have its own fighting knife produced it would be similar to the F-S.

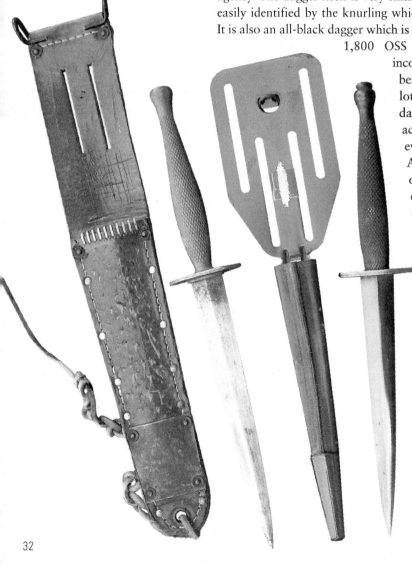

Two direct US descendants of the F-S dagger: on the left is the USMC Raider stiletto and on the right the OSS stiletto. Note the "pancake flapper" sheath for the OSS stiletto.

Since the OSS stiletto was a full-sized knife, it was probably intended primarily for use by OSS Operational Groups, the paramilitary arm of the agency. The dagger itself is very similar to a 2nd Pattern F-S, though it is easily identified by the knurling which extends down to the crossguard. It is also an all-black dagger which is "sterile" with no markings. The first 1,800 OSS blades were allegedly tempered incorrectly, and hence had a tendency to bend and break. As a result, that entire lot was rejected. However, these OSS daggers were later re-inspected and, according to John Brunner, 1,728 were eventually accepted for OSS issue. By August 1943, all 10,000 OSS stilettos ordered had been delivered. The dot encountered on OSS stilettos near the crossguard shows that the blade was given the Brinell hardness test. Two Brinell dots indicate that a blade was originally tested and rejected, then re-hardened.

Far more distinctive is the OSS dagger's sheath, known by collectors as the "pancake flapper." This description is actually quite appropriate, as the household manufacturing firm of Landers, Ferry, & Clark, which produced the sheath, stamped the metal belt loop portion from a sheet of olive-drab steel using dies for one of the company's spatulas. The sheath's chape was stamped from the same steel sheet. Reportedly, Fairbairn liked the OSS sheath and carried his personal F-S knife in a "pancake flapper." It is possible that the

feature Fairbairn liked about the sheath – given his favored technique for bringing the blade into action, based on Shanghai experiments – was the versatility in carry methods, especially with the sheath slanted on the "support side" for a quick draw and presentation of the knife.

Most researchers and collectors attribute the fabrication of the OSS dagger to Landers, Ferry, & Clark as well as the sheath; however, some believe the knives were made on order in the UK. This confusion may result from the fact that the OSS considered purchasing daggers in the UK but found that the price quoted by Landers, Ferry, & Clark was substantially less.

The description of the OSS stiletto given in the restricted manual of OSS weapons is interesting:

DESCRIPTION: The high grade steel blade is diamond shaped in cross section from the hilt to the point. The hilt, handle, and knob are made of three separate pieces of brass which are assembled securely onto the blade. The Knife is carried in a special scabbard, designed so that it may be worn high or low on the belt. By using one upper and one lower slot the scabbard may be angled into any position, fitted snugly to any part of the body, with ready access to either hand.

PURPOSE: The Fighting Knife is a close combat weapon, excellent for stealthy attack, but it is not designed for all-purpose use. It may supplement firearms or be used by the operator as his sole means of defense or offense. The knife is double-edged and can be used for either penetration or cutting.

The OSS Training Cadre which included William Fairbairn first row, second from right, and Rex Applegate, last row, fourth from left. (Rex Applegate)

V-42: The Black Devil's Brigade stiletto

Although it is least like the F-S dagger in configuration, the most interesting US World War II "stiletto" is the V-42, designed for the 1st Special Service Force, a joint US/Canadian unit trained for winter warfare in anticipation of raiding missions in Norway. Force members were among the most elite of US units and are considered the true forerunners of today's US special forces. Like the Commandos, the 1st Special Service Force, known colloquially as the "Black Devil's Brigade," was trained in close combat by a former Shanghai Municipal Police officer, Dermot "Pat" O'Neill.

The V-42 stiletto was designed with input from various Force officers, some of whom were familiar with the F-S from having observed or taken part in Commando training in the UK. Once the desired features were agreed upon, specifications were submitted to Case Cutlery for prototypes. Officially designated "Fighting Commando Knife, Type V-42," it is generally known as the "V-42 stiletto" or the 1st Special Service Force knife.

Killing with the V-42

This close-up of the classic carotid thrusts taught to World War II special forces is delivered by a member of the US 1st Special Service Force on one of the night raids that this unit carried out, killing German soldiers and leaving calling cards to dishearten the survivors. Severing the carotid artery could be expected to cause unconsciousness in five seconds and death in 12 seconds. This thrust was the second-fastest way to kill using an artery strike (after the subclavian thrust, see page 43), but the carotid was closer to the surface and more vulnerable. Note that the Force man grabs the helmet to pull the head back, exposing the carotid – a technique favored by "Pat" O'Neill, the unit's close combat instructor who had served with Fairbairn in Shanghai. On occasion the skull-crusher pommel of the V-42 – unique among F-S-type Commando daggers – could also be used to inflict a fast and less bloody death.

Although specifications for each knife might vary slightly due to hand grinding and assembly, the typical V-42 has a 7$\frac{7}{16}$in double-edged "stiletto" blade. This blade was double-hollow ground, resulting in an excellent edge. On the ricasso, it had a ridged "fingerprint" which helped position the thumb for some of the blade techniques taught to Force men. The crossguard curved downward and had a leather backing to cushion it against the hand. Stacked leather washers formed the handle, and a pointed "skull crusher" formed the pommel. The V-42 sheath is instantly recognizable from its 20in length; reportedly, this was specified because the Force's cold weather mission would entail wearing parkas, and a longer sheath (with the knife therefore further down the leg) would allow easier access. As with the Raider stiletto, many V-42 sheaths had staples along the front of the mouth. The sheath also had a leather tie-down thong and a snap retention strap. Some 1st Special Service Force members used a carry method for their V-42s similar to that of the Marine Raiders,

The OSS stiletto in action

In this scene a member of OSS Detachment 101 working with the Kachins in Burma hears a Japanese point man approaching down a jungle trail. Assuming he will be discovered if he fires his .45cal pistol or M1 carbine, he waits until the Japanese soldier's arm comes past with rifle pointed forward and delivers two quick slashes to the brachial and radial arteries, stunning the Japanese and causing him to drop his weapon. With the soldier disarmed and in pain, the OSS man can step in to finish him. The danger is, of course, that the Japanese will call out; however, had he been allowed to discover the OSS man, he would have almost certainly cried out or fired. With just the slashes already delivered the Japanese will lose consciousness in 30 seconds or less. Note the OSS stiletto and distinctive OSS sheath worn by the Detachment 101 operative.

On the outskirts of Rome, LtGen Mark Clark confers with other general officers including BrigGen Robert T. Fredericks, former commander of the 1st Special Service Force. Note that Fredericks (far right) continues to wear his V-42 "Force" dagger. (NARA 111-SCA-4402)

with the knife mounted behind their pistol holsters. Sgt Joe Dauphinais of 1st Special Service Force remembered vividly the V-42 stiletto, and the intensity of O'Neill's blade training:

> The V-42 stiletto is a very impressive blade. When you hold it in your hand it is as if it were alive. O'Neill had us practicing on each other with our blades all of the time.

The original order to Case for V-42s was for 1,750 knives. At least one additional order was placed, bringing the total ordered to at least 3,000. However, since more than 6,000 men eventually served in the 1st Special Service Force, there may have also been one or more additional orders.

Members of 1st Special Service Force were quite proud of the V-42, to the extent that many sent them home so they did not get lost or damaged in combat! This probably accounts for the very nice examples sometimes encountered.

1st Special Service Force V-42 stiletto; note the long sheath for wear under Arctic clothing and the skull crusher pommel. (Jeff Knox)

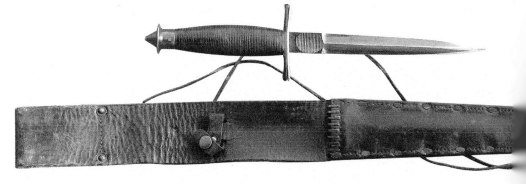

USE
Fighting Hitler with cold steel

TRAINING FOR COMBAT

The development of the ideal fighting knife, whether for Shanghai policemen or World War II Commandos, was worth little without effective training in its use. During World War I, the prevalence of trench combat had engendered substantial interest in knife-fighting technique and specialized "trench knives." However, between the wars, few military units continued to emphasize the fighting knife. Instead, bayonet training prepared troops for the use of "cold steel" at the end of their rifles. The development of elite raiding units during World War II, however, rehabilitated the fighting knife both as a silent killing weapon and as a symbol of aggressiveness.

The Fairbairn-Sykes dagger was a pure fighting knife, and to be used most effectively in combat, its wielder needed instruction in quick and deadly techniques to employ its edge, point, and pommel against an enemy. Special forces instructors such as Fairbairn, Sykes, O'Neill, and Applegate developed a training regime designed to give their students both the physical and psychological skills needed to use their Commando daggers to deadly effect.

It is very important not to misunderstand the psychological importance of knife training. When the author received his first training in close combat with the blade, it was stressed that there would be a lot of blood and that if fighting is blade-to-blade, everyone will get cut! Fairbairn and the other instructors had to take prospective Commandos or SOE and OSS operators and turn them from civilians into killers with deadly weapons – although to paraphrase some of Fairbairn's philosophy, there are no deadly weapons, only deadly men (and, in OSS and SOE, women). Incidentally, Fairbairn's own daughter Dorothea, who helped in the preparation of his book *Self Defense for Women*, served in SOE herself. OSS trainees at the Camp X training school in Canada found Fairbairn's close combat training especially eye-opening. During the war, OSS was sometimes sarcastically said to stand for "Oh So Social" because many of the recruits were graduates of Ivy League schools who came from wealth and privilege or academia. This was true, but in the defense of OSS, these were often the Americans who had language skills and who had spent substantial time abroad.

Close combat instructors had not only to teach their trainees, often in a matter of days, the most effective techniques for using their daggers, but also to instill the willingness to close with an enemy, grapple with him, and messily take his life. If possible, it is best to incapacitate or kill the opponent with a surprise thrust deep into a critical part of the body. This single devastating wound is the ideal basis for sentry elimination. Good blade training helps overcome potential squeamishness, by making the necessary actions automatic. Fairbairn felt, too, that the knowledge that one had a good knife such as the F-S and the skills to use it gave an agent or Commando great confidence when the knife came out of the sheath, especially in the dark.

Much of the training with the F-S dagger took place at the Commando Training Centre, Achnacarry, Scotland, the SOE training facility at Arisaig, Scotland, the OSS Training Facility Area F (actually the Congressional Country Club in Potomac, MD), or Camp X. An interesting F-S anecdote told by former instructors and students at Camp X is that sentries there attempted to appear unarmed and pass as local civilians, although they didn't really fool many locals! These sentries, many reportedly survivors

Lord Lovat, the tall officer third from right, briefs his Commandos prior to training for a raid. Note the dagger worn tucked into flaps on the battle dress trousers of the Commando at right. (IWM H18951)

of the Dieppe raid, carried F-S daggers in hidden sheaths designed to fasten inside the trousers to the suspender buttons common at the time.

Although each close combat instructor added certain twists of their own to the training (Sykes reportedly ended each demonstration with the words, "Then kick him in the balls!"), much of the training was based upon Fairbairn's techniques of blade usage. Among the basic tenets Fairbairn taught were the following:

1. There is no one perfect stance for knife fighting since terrain and other conditions will vary, but a crouch with knees and waist flexible for balance and quick movement is desirable.

2. The best grip is with the hilt resting on the index finger and with the other fingers wrapped comfortably around the hilt. Generally, the knife is held relatively loosely by the fingers other than the thumb and index finger which grip tightly; however, when delivering a thrust or a slash to the left, the fingers tighten to give a strong grip. Fairbairn had various exercises to give the trainee confidence in handling the knife. These included delivering cuts by whipping the knife to the right or left, moving the knife in a Figure 8, various slashes including a quick double right–left or left–right slash, thrusts (preferably throat thrusts) incorporating a forward lunge off the right foot (for right-handed trainees), and circular slashes in which the trainee jumped and turned the body while delivering a powerful slash with the knife.

3. The fighting knife may be used for offense or defense. On offense when the knife is not already drawn, Fairbairn stressed that the forearm of the non-knife hand should cover the knife hand so the enemy does not see that the knife being drawn. The preferred move upon the draw is to spring towards the enemy slashing at his face, as even if the slash does not strike home it will rock the enemy back off balance. Fairbairn taught trainees the position of major arteries and emphasized the importance of attacking them. Generally, he would discuss the time until loss of consciousness and death occurs when each artery is slashed. For Commando training in sentry elimination, Fairbairn attached great importance to grabbing an enemy by the head, hand over mouth, twisting the head to the left, then deep thrusting into the carotid followed by slashing sideways. Unconsciousness would normally result within five seconds. Fairbairn also stressed the powerful downward thrust into the subclavian artery in the shoulder which would normally result in unconsciousness in two seconds. For OSS or SOE agents there was one consideration for silent killing which for the Commandos, Rangers, SAS, and other uniformed special forces units was less critical. When agents used the blade, they also had to consider the amount of blood which was likely to spurt as they delivered their thrusts or slashes, as blood on their clothing could attract attention leading to their capture.

Royal Canadian Navy Beach Commandos practising close combat techniques with their Commando daggers. Fairbairn and other Commando instructors stressed realistic training with bare blades. (Lt Gilbert A. Milne/Canada Dept of National Defense/Library and Archives Canada/PA-183022)

Agents remembered Fairbairn's discussions of silent killing and blood well:[3]

At Area B, Fairbairn taught his lethal hand-to-hand fighting technique, and also how to handle the Fairbairn-Sykes fighting knife, a razor-sharp stiletto of his personal design. "The knife is a silent, deadly weapon. It's great for sentries. Never mind the blood. Just take care of it quickly." After completing a course in knife fighting, the new students took a course in unarmed "Gutter Fighting." "In a sense, this is for fools, because you should never be without a pistol or a knife. However, in case you are caught unarmed, foolishly or otherwise, the tactics shown here will increase your chances of coming out alive."

Fairbairn believed in the necessity of making close combat training realistic:

[3] The following extracts are taken from Patrick O'Donnell, *Operatives, Spies, and Saboteurs.*

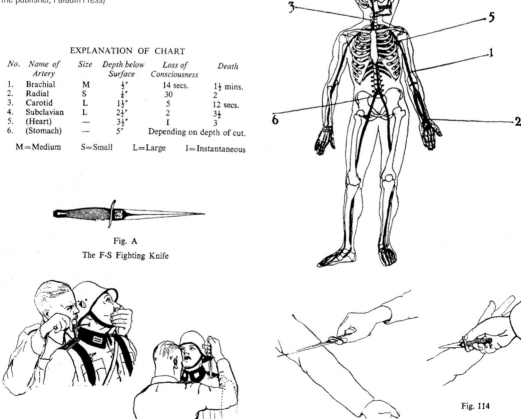

EXPLANATION OF CHART

No.	Name of Artery	Size	Depth below Surface	Loss of Consciousness	Death
1.	Brachial	M	½″	14 secs.	1½ mins.
2.	Radial	S	¼″	30	2
3.	Carotid	L	1½″	5	12 secs.
4.	Subclavian	L	2½″	2	3½
5.	(Heart)	—	3½″	I	3
6.	(Stomach)	—	5″	Depending on depth of cut.	

M = Medium   S = Small   L = Large   I = Instantaneous

Fig. A
The F-S Fighting Knife

Fig. 115

Fig. 116

Fig. 113

Fig. 114

Realistic training was a hallmark for the OSS Commandos, who worked in units called Operational Groups (OGs). The OGs received most of their training on the lavish 18-hole Congressional Country Club, known as Area F. "Aggressiveness of spirit and willingness to close with the enemy were stressed," so OG training was designed to be as close to reality as possible… "Major Fairbairn trained us in knife fighting and hand-to-hand combat. Tragically, a private accidentally killed another private during a simulation."

Fairbairn made it clear that, for an unarmed man, defending against the knife is extremely difficult. When facing a knife with a knife, the agent or Commando should keep moving and concentrate on the enemy's knife; rather than approaching the enemy, the trainee should allow the attacker to come to him, and then he should evade or counter the enemy's thrust before closing. The enemy's knife arm should be attacked by slashing, and grappling on the ground should be avoided. Another tenet of Fairbairn's school of fighting was that distance is the best defense against a knife and should be used when possible.

He was also a great believer that when doing firearms training trainees should go through a "house of horrors" in which they would have to react quickly and engage various targets as they passed through a darkened shooting area. For blade training, he liked to use what he called shadow-fighting, in which trainees were given a scenario such as infiltrating an enemy installation. With drawn knife, they would move through an area in low light and, using their F-S, be required to counter "attacks" as the instructor called out the direction from which the "attack" was coming. The shadow-fighting scenarios became more difficult later in the course, when they were carried out in wooded areas over uneven ground. Such exercises built reaction time and confidence in handling the knife quickly.

The Commandos' use of bare blades during training seems to have been a technique for giving their soldiers both a healthy respect for an enemy with a knife, and also confidence should they have to face a blade. It is a uniquely unnerving sensation to face an enemy wielding a fighting knife, and it was important to ensure that a Commando's first experience of this was not in mortal combat. The Commandos were great believers in the military adage "Sweat in training saves blood in combat," though occasionally they shed a bit of blood in training as well! Able Seaman George Fagence of H Naval Commando, one of the beachhead coordination specialists of the Royal Naval Commandos, told of a near miss with the F-S, which hammered home the deadliness of the dagger:

This weapon was carried as a last resort. I do know it lived up to its reputation, as during practice I accidentally stuck it into Florrie Ford's back and he went down like a sack of chaff. It's OK – he lived.[4]

Although a leap from on high to deliver a subclavian or other thrust with the Commando dagger would rarely be used, this Royal Navy Beach Commando certainly trains to use his blade with enthusiasm! (IWM A17757)

[4] Quoted in David Lee, *Beachhead Assault*

Blade training today takes place using training knives with blunt point and edges, sometimes with chalk or lipstick applied to the edges so that "hits" can be determined at the end of training. The author has not found any reference to Fairbairn or the other instructors using training knives; however, he has seen at least one Commando dagger with a blunt point and edges, which appears to have been used for training purposes. In *British and Commonwealth Military Knives*, Ron Flook illustrates a training 3rd Pattern Commando dagger with a blunt tip that retracts into the hollow blade during a strike.

A hostile beach

A member of COPPs (Combined Operations Pilotage Parties) has come ashore to survey a French beach and encountered a Vichy soldier on patrol. Normally, the COPPists wanted to avoid detection and, hence, would not want to leave a dead body. However, should his partner offshore in a Folbot kayak face discovery or the sentry block his path back to the ocean, he might eliminate the sentry. Should the beach being surveyed be intended as a ruse to distract attention from Normandy, leaving a dead sentry and some beach survey equipment might even be desirable!

An interesting comment on the effectiveness of the blade techniques taught by Fairbairn is that the Germans managed to obtain a copy of a publication illustrating Fairbairn's close combat techniques. For propaganda purposes, they reprinted certain sections in a pamphlet to illustrate how "vicious" the Allied special forces were; they then distributed this pamphlet in occupied countries, and perhaps some neutral ones.

Training in the use of the F-S dagger as a pure fighting knife doesn't mean that troops did not also misuse it. Soldiers find many uses for knives; opening cans, prying open crates, even entertaining themselves by throwing

The French Resistance

This scene portrays a pair of French Resistance fighters who have encountered a member of the Vichy Milice and been compromised by having their SOE clandestine radio exposed. Thinking quickly, the female has thrown her arms around the Milice to prevent him bringing his MAS-38 submachine gun into action. The male

Resistance fighter has drawn his Commando dagger and is delivering a deep thrust to the subclavian artery while punching the Milice in the face at the same time to distract him. His dagger is of the all-steel type used by Free French and French Resistance fighters.

them at trees. The F-S did not really lend itself to those endeavors. Commandos were also issued a clasp knife, but they still often misused their F-S. Troops with a parachute mission who were issued F-S daggers or who purchased their own found that they were not ideal for cutting lines in tight quarters. Some Rangers or Commandos found, too, that the F-S was sometimes a bit long for use aboard crowded small boats. COPPs swimmers (the men of the Combined Operations Assault Pilotage Parties, the swimmers and canoeists who specialized in carrying out clandestine hydrographic surveys of beaches prior to the Allied landings) often purchased some of the smaller clandestine knives available from cutlers for use in their underwater missions – some in rubber sheaths that could completely cover the knife while swimming. Nor did the Commandos just learn to use their blades to eliminate Germans. Part of their training was in field butchery so they could live off the land if necessary. Once again, the F-S was not at its best for this task, though according to several sources Anders Lassen, who won a Victoria Cross while serving with the Special Boat Squadron of the SAS, would stalk and kill deer in the Highlands with his F-S while undergoing Commando training. As part of the Small Scale Raiding Force, during an October 1942 raid on the island of Sark, Lassen put these same skills to use stalking and killing a German sentry.

This Commando carries his 1st Pattern F-S dagger on his left side but also carries a Smatchet, another weapon highly favored by Fairbairn. (IWM H17461)

The Marine Raiders found that they did not like their Raider stilettos for many of the same reasons. The Raiders considered the balance poor, probably because of the change in handle material. These handles had a tendency to deteriorate and begin cracking, while the Raiders managed to break many of the blades. Often the breakage was through misuse such as throwing the stiletto at palm trees to counteract boredom. Nevertheless, the Marines actually preferred their Ka-Bar utility fighting knives since they stood up to abuse and made good utility knives, yet still served well against the Japanese in night-time close combat, and were readily replaced through the supply system if broken or lost.

OSS agents found – as with other versions of the F-S – that the tip of their dagger's blade had a tendency to break. Another problem encountered by OSS agents was the loss of the dagger from its sheath during the impact of parachute landings, in some cases causing the knife to injure its owner.

Even as a pure combat knife, the F-S displayed certain flaws to the Commandos and others using it. The sharply pointed stiletto blade had a tendency to break off, either through misuse or combat use, leaving the user with a knife minus its first half-inch or so of blade. This was easily remedied by grinding a new point, which was often done. As a result, it is very common for collectors to find 1st and 2nd Pattern F-S daggers with blades up to an inch shorter than standard. Knives that lost their tips and were reground were actually much stronger than undamaged examples.

Another area where flaws were noticed was the coke-bottle-shaped grip, which had a tendency to turn in the hand during use. Also, if the knife was grasped hurriedly with no time to feel the crossguard, the shape of the grip did not orientate the hand by feel alone – so when the knife was required quickly, its user could not always orientate it for correct use. To fix one or both of these problems, Commandos and other users sometimes ground a flat on the two sides of the F-S handle so that the flat spot was aligned with the blade's spine. The flats oriented the blade correctly in the dark, and also kept the blade from turning so easily in the hand. Collectors occasionally encounter what would be a desirable F-S variation were the handle not ground in what is usually an unsightly manner, but the grinding often indicates that the knife belonged to someone who really used it.

COMBAT USE DURING WORLD WAR II

First blood

Units such as the Commandos must be used, to keep the troops motivated and to fulfill their mission of harassing the enemy and building morale at home. The earliest Commando raid, in the area around Boulogne, was carried out on June 23/24, 1940, the very night France surrendered. Another raid was carried out on Guernsey on the night of July 14/15, 1940. These early raids were mostly symbolic but did allow the fledgling Commandos to learn a few lessons. From 1941, however, missions became bolder. One of the earliest combat deployments of the F-S was during Operation *Colossus*, the airborne raid of February 10, 1941, against the Tragino aqueduct near Calitri in southern Italy.

The early airborne troops who jumped during Operation *Colossus* had been drawn from 2 Commando and hence were trained with the new 1st Pattern F-S knife. In this first British airborne operation, the troops followed the German practice of jumping without their heavier weapons: their Thompson submachine guns and Bren guns being dropped in containers. For the jump, the paratroopers were armed only with their F-S knives and .32cal Colt automatic pistols. Once the aqueduct had been blown up, the paratroopers were to attempt to reach the Italian coast for a submarine pickup. They moved at night and hid during the day. Just before dawn, one of the groups of paratroopers was preparing to hide for the day in a fruit orchard when an Italian farm worker passed them. Lt Jowett drew his F-S dagger and

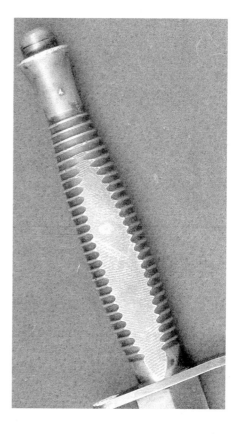

To prevent the Commando dagger turning in the hand some World War II users ground flats on each side of the handle. (Jeff Knox)

Cpl Aubrey of the SBS sharpens his Commando dagger prior to a mission. (IWM E29095)

prepared to use the silent killing skills he had learned at Achnacarry, but the worker disappeared into the darkness, and it was decided not to pursue him and to take cover before daylight. Thus passed the chance to make one of the first kills of the war with the F-S!

George Peel of 3 Commando did, however, put his training into practice, during the Vaagso raid. The training given by Fairbairn and other instructors to instill quick reactions in close combat paid off, as Peel reports:

> We moved forward, using house-to-house techniques, diving into porches, our Lee-Enfield rifles at the ready. I was in a doorway and I had a feeling, the door behind me opened slowly. When it was half open, I gave it a kick and standing there was a German officer. Without even having to think, I whipped my knife out and stabbed him. But then I couldn't bring myself to pull it out of him. It suddenly appalled me what I'd done. For all the training we'd had – and it was the reaction I'd been trained for – this was one of the worst episodes of my career.[5]

Commando close combat training was designed to remove the hesitation or squeamishness Peel felt after the fact. When a threat presented itself, Peel was trained to react quickly without thought – training which probably saved his life, since in the doorway it was unlikely he could have quickly brought his rifle to bear.

[5] Quoted in Niall Cherry, *Striking Back*

Only two F-S knives were taken on Operation *Freshman*, the November 1942 failed glider-borne assault on the Norwegian heavy water plant. The two men who were issued the knives were Lt A. Allen and Lt D. Methven, who were the commanding officers in each of the two gliders. Methven died during the crash landing of his glider, while Allen was murdered by the Germans under Hitler's "Commando Order," which instructed that any Allied Commandos captured, even in uniform, should be executed immediately. It was generally accepted that the fear engendered by British Commandos and their use of the F-S knife on German troops was one factor in the issuance of this order.

Although silent killing was the best way to take out a sentry, it was often preferable to avoid leaving bodies which might attract attention before the raiders had departed. Special forces troops would frequently prepare to use their F-S knives on an intended Italian or German victim, but would allow him to survive because he did not recognize the men for British raiders. One such incident occurred when the SAS was raiding airfields near Benghazi. Sgt Rose related the details:

> About five minutes later we came to a roadblock with an Italian sentry on guard, so we had to halt. Captain "Fitzroy" Maclean spoke to him sharply in Italian while Cooper and I got our knives out ready for a spot of bother; he wasn't very inquisitive though and we got away without any trouble.[6]

Later, they had to return past the same sentry and while Capt Maclean talked their way through, they were ready with their daggers to eliminate the Italian if necessary. He narrowly escaped death by F-S dagger twice! In his case not being particularly alert kept him alive.

Marine Raiders: knife-fighting in the Pacific

The US Marine 2nd Raider Battalion trained with stilettos and other blades during the lead up to the raid on Makin Atoll in the Gilbert Islands on August 17–18, 1942. Although the raid was designed to gather intelligence and divert attention from the landings on Guadalcanal and Tulagi, it also served – as did Commando raids against the European coast – to show Americans that US forces were on the offensive against the Axis. The Japanese had a seaplane base and 70–80 personnel on the atoll. The 2nd Marine Raider Battalion launched in rubber boats from submarines and landed with difficulty. The Raiders killed most of the garrison, with estimates of Japanese dead ranging from 60 to over 100. The Marines lost 12 killed and 12 missing in action, of which nine were left behind and executed by the Japanese. The Raiders took no prisoners and captured little if any intelligence but the raid received much publicity in the USA and was a morale builder. In addition, the Japanese strengthened their island bases throughout the area in fear of other raids, thus tying down troops that could have been used on Guadalcanal or elsewhere.

[6] Quoted in Malcolm James, *Born of the Desert*

Each Raider was issued two knives, a stiletto type and a heartier Jim Bowie type. Knife and bayonet experts were invited to Jacques Farm to share their expertise. An emphasis was placed on close-in combat and where best to demobilize an enemy. The men took their knife training seriously: "It was dangerous to walk around at night because you might be hit by someone throwing a knife at a tree." Brian Quirk remembered. "We had a lot of young crazy guys in the outfit."[7]

Of course, knife throwing practice of this type was one of the reasons so many Marine Raider stilettos were broken. The "Bowie type" knife referred to is probably the Collins No.18 Machete which had a Bowie-style 9½in blade and which was issued to the Raiders.

During the raid on Makin Atoll, the Raiders got a chance to use their stilettos on the enemy. Raider "Killer" Wygal

> ... crawled around our right flank, along the shoreline of the Lagoon, and saw a lot of dead Japs – and the live ones he was after. Huddled back of a water-cooled machine gun, they were raking our lines. Using hand grenades, his pistol, and his knife, Wygal sent those Nips to their ancestors.[8]

Also on Makin, Sgt Buck Stidham learned the value of the quick reactions with his stiletto that he had gained in training when he came upon a group of Japanese bodies:

> They were the first enemy I had seen, and I let curiosity overrule my common sense as I knelt beside one and started examining him for souvenirs. To my surprise the "dead" Jap suddenly groaned and raised up on his knees. Fortunately, I had a knife wedged down in my pistol holster, so I whipped it out and punctured his lung.[9]

Members of the 1st Raider Battalion had a slightly different view of their blade usage, though they agreed with other Raiders that the stiletto was too fragile to use as an all-round knife:

> Edson's Raiders did not use the oversized Bowie blades – the "Gung Ho knives" – that became the trademark of Carlson's 2nd Raider Battalion. For awhile Edson's men carried the special USMC stiletto, a stabbing knife with a seven-inch blade manufactured by Camillus Cutlery and modeled after the Fairbairn-Sykes design made popular by the British Commandos. The Raiders found the Marine stiletto to be well suited for silent killing but little use for anything else. Later in 1943 they would gratefully welcome the arrival of the ubiquitous Ka-Bar, the all-purpose field combat knife, lethal enough for hand-to-hand fighting, sturdy enough for campcraft jobs – opening rations

48   [7, 8 & 9] George W. Smith, *Carlson's Raid*

cutting tent pegs, even digging an emergency foxhole or latrine. The stiletto was too frail for any of these common tasks.[10]

It is interesting that even though the 1st Raider Battalion found fault with their stilettos, they still called hit-and-run raiding missions against the Japanese "stiletto operations"! At least one Raider of the 1st Raider Battalion survived the fighting for "Raiders' Ridge" on Guadalcanal because of this stiletto. Cpl Gene Eleston reported that after his machine gun crew had been overwhelmed, a mêlée ensued:

> We just bumped into each other. It was black as pitch. But I knew he was my enemy and he knew I was his. From the direction he was coming there weren't any Marines.

Knife fighting does not come naturally to most men, but Eleston was struggling for his life:

> We grappled. He was smaller, but stocky. He was strong. He was brave – They all were brave.

[10] Joseph H. Alexander, *Edson's Raiders*

Landing on Butaritari Island, Makin Atoll, from the submarine *Nautilus*, the Raiders were lightly equipped and lost entire boats of weapons and gear in the treacherous conditions. Despite the confusion, most of the Raiders achieved their objectives thanks to their discipline and preparation. Highly trained but lightly armed, the Raiders made notable use of their famous stilettos on Makin. (Artwork by Howard Gerrard, © Osprey Publishing)

Eleston's stiletto prevailed but the memory haunted him:

One of my nightmares; he comes without a face.[11]

COPPs swimmers, who landed clandestinely on enemy beaches to do surveys prior to landings, initially carried a .38cal Enfield revolver and an F-S but later switched to a Government Model .45cal automatic. They took care to waterproof their weapons as much as possible and thoroughly cleaned and lubricated them after each mission. The swimmers were often alone on an enemy beach and sometimes penetrated far enough inland to check local defenses. Their F-S daggers were their first choice for eliminating an enemy sentry or a guard dog quietly. However, some COPPs parties were eventually issued the Welrod .32cal automatic pistol for silent sentry elimination. Many felt the F-S was surer.

Members of COPPs received their blade training from Bruce Ogden Smith of the Special Boat Section. Smith was held in awe by the COPPs trainees as rumor had it that he had used his F-S to dispatch a German SS man. Whether the story was true or not, they paid close attention to Smith's instruction.

The importance that the members of COPPs attached to their F-S daggers is graphically illustrated by the symbol of the COPPs Association – a dolphin leaping behind a Commando dagger.

Commando invasion: raids and landings in Europe

Later in the war, the Commandos were in the vanguard of the wave of assaults and landings that would eventually lead the Allied armies to the heart of the Reich. From Sicily to the south of France and the Normandy landings themselves, Commandos were used for reconnaissance, sabotage, and small unit operations. As they frequently patrolled hostile territory unsupported and in small groups, the ability to kill reliably in complete silence was often vital to their survival.

The Royal Naval Commandos, or "Beach Commandos," not only completed specialized Royal Navy training for coordinating operations across beaches but also attended the Commando course at Achnacarry. Generally, they carried F-S daggers and a handgun while operating on darkened enemy beaches. Although RN Commandos were always ready to use their knives against any Germans they might encounter, on January 22, 1944, during the Anzio landings, they found a novel use for their F-S daggers.

A minefield was encountered on the beach, which brought the DUKW amphibious trucks delivering troops to a stop. Army sappers had landed on the wrong beach, so the RN Commandos drew their daggers and crawled along the beach, probing with them for the wooden-cased mines which would defeat mine detectors. Not only did the RN Commandos mark a path through the minefield but they recovered dead and wounded troops who had fallen prey to the mines.

[11] Joseph H. Alexander, *Edson's Raiders*

They seemed to take particularly well to the knife training the Commando course offered, perhaps because they thought it might stand them in good stead on a darkened beach one day. RN Commandos were quite proud of their F-S knives and green berets, which they were awarded upon completion of Commando training, although many continued to wear Royal Navy headgear.

Members of the 2nd Battalion, Parachute Regiment after a drop on Depienne in December 1942. Note the F-S dagger worn by the officer on the right. (IWM NA351)

At Anzio, one unit which made excellent use of their fighting knives, as intended, was the 1st Special Service Force. Various Force members remember their use of the V-42 against the Germans.[12] Sgt Bill Story related memories of "Pat" O'Neill's training of the Force with the V-42:

He [O'Neill] also taught us how to use our V-42. The V-42 has a thumbprint on the top of the blade to keep the blade flat. It had to be flat because it had to slide in through the ribs when going for the heart. If you didn't, the blade could get stuck in the ribs and you'd cut into the bone or cartilage, and then you couldn't get it out. O'Neill also taught us how to reverse the knife quickly to use the skull crusher on either temple, the most vulnerable place. Another technique was coming up behind a guy, grabbing his helmet, pulling his head back, and using the knife to cut his throat. But you must realize that it's one thing to train and talk about what you're going to do to the enemy and quite another to take a guy who is no older than you are, maybe even younger, and do this to him – even if he's wearing a different uniform.

---

[12] Quotations from Story, McNeese, and Kaisner are taken from *The Black Devil Brigade*, the oral history of the unit, assembled by Joseph A. Springer

Famous Commando officer "Mad Jack" Churchill examines a captured 75mm gun. His F-S dagger, which appears to be a 1st Pattern, is on his hip. Churchill was known to like cold steel and often carried his claymore and bow and arrows on operations. (IWM N463)

At Anzio the training and familiarity with the V-42 paid off. Sgt Gil McNeese remembered night patrols against German positions:

> We began going out every night in small teams, working behind German lines and knocking off as many positions as possible. Everyone had their own technique for doing this. Many used their knives, some used their Tommyguns, and others used their bare hands. Capt Pat O'Neill, our hand-to-hand combat instructor, would ask a Kraut for a cigarette in German, and when the Kraut answered, Pat would shoot him once in the face with a Tommygun, because it was pretty quiet when firing one shot. Then he would move on to the next position. They didn't expect anyone that deep in their lines except another Kraut…
>
> O'Neill didn't believe in the over-the-head slash; he attacked from behind while holding the knife down low. You can't defend against that. We would go for the kidney, too. I know of one instance when one of our guys used the skull crusher on a Kraut sentry, behind his ear, just to see what would happen. It was instant – very quiet and very quick.
>
> We would do this almost every night. We carried death stickers and would put these on their foreheads. One was the Force spearhead. The one I used was "DAS DICKE ENDE KOMMT NOCH" which means, It's only going to get worse, or something like that. Another we used said "Beware! the FSSF will get you next!" We messed with their heads on so many different levels.

Probing for mines (previous pages)

During the invasion of Sicily on a beachhead near Gela, a Royal Navy Beach Commando uses his Commando dagger to expose a German S-Mine ("Bouncing Betty"). As the barbed wire cannot be cut or removed because Italian "Red Devil" grenades with trip wires have been set as booby traps, he is trying to probe a way through the minefield so that troops can get off the beach.

SSgt Victor Kaisner also remembered putting the V-42 to good use at Anzio:

> We used our knives many times. This was the way to do it because it was usually quiet. And we were trained for this. This was what it was all about. We would just sneak up and get a hold of their helmets and cut their throats. For example, we went out one night, we made a little noise, their machine gun took off, we held our fire, and I sent the men forward. I could actually hear the Kraut trying to say "*Schwartzer Teufel*" [Black Devil] as they were slicing his throat. Then they gave him a sticker. But that really surprised us that he knew who was killing him.

Some life and death struggles required the use of the F-S. During a July 1944 raid on Crete, with the mission to destroy German fuel dumps, a Pte Stewart was attempting to escape after laying his demolition charges. He was crawling through the wire when a German sentry jumped on top of him, shouting. "We struggled for some time," said Stewart. "After a while, I managed to draw my knife. I put it in his stomach and he fell, but still shouting."[13]

Commandos and agents were trained to use their blades when maintaining silence was necessary to avoid compromising a mission. As a result, the blades were often drawn when it appeared that it would be imminently necessary to eliminate a threat, even when the silent kill was not carried out. Ian Wellsted's small reconnaissance party of SAS troops had jumped into occupied France on June 6, 1944, to link up with the French Resistance and prepare the way for additional SAS jeep patrols to be inserted. Once landed on the drop zone, Wellsted was assigned to guard their equipment while the other team members retrieved their radios or checked the area. Wellsted describes the incident as follows:

> All of a sudden I heard footsteps coming heavily down the road. I did not want to use the Colt that I carried for fear of the noise. I drew my knife. I have never liked the idea of knifing a man. It has always struck me as rather messy, but it looked as though there wasn't much option this time. I gripped the hilt hard and waited. Then softly I heard a voice. "Gremlin are you there?" Denby had returned with Gapeau but Centime could not be found.[14]

This incident illustrates various aspects of F-S use on clandestine operations. First, training had given troops and agents sufficient confidence in their ability to use the dagger that they were prepared to employ it when the tactical situation seemed to require it. Note also that as Wellsted prepared to use his dagger, he gripped it tightly in the manner Fairbairn taught for delivering a deep thrust.

A member of the SAS in the Western Desert wears shorts and sandals but keeps his 1st Pattern F-S dagger close at hand. (IWM E21344)

[13] Incident related in John Lodwick's book on the wartime SBS, *The Filibusters*
[14] Ian Wellstead, *SAS with the Maquis*

Although the F-S was designed as a pure fighting knife, there are many ways to misuse it. Slicing cheese was among the more harmless. (IWM H38952)

Wellsted found other uses for his F-S while living in the woods with the Maquis. In discussing their cooking arrangements, he states:

> At first we were handicapped by no real cooking utensils, but cans for boiling water and brewing tea were improvised out of parachute containers and empty biscuit tins, and to the end of our stay in the woods we continued to cook over open fires with these makeshift pots and pans. Our fighting knives came in very useful for cutting and for opening tins, and clean or not-so-clean sticks were used for stirring.

Sometimes managing to retain their Commando daggers while going into action proved a problem. Pte R. Scott was among the paratroopers on the Bruneval raid, the mission to parachute into occupied France to seize a German radar station, and escape by sea with the equipment and captured technicians. He tells of what happened when exiting the Whitley aircraft:

> I was Number 6 in the stick and in the descent just before leaving the Whitley I was clobbered by a container [dropped containing equipment for the raid] and didn't I just curse the RAF dispatcher. On landing I found that my fighting knife had gone and my trouser leg was ripped down the seam.[15]

---

[15] Quoted in Niall Cherry, *Striking Back*. This may indicate that Pte Scott had his dagger affixed with the two flaps attached to his battle dress and buttoned over the F-S sheath.

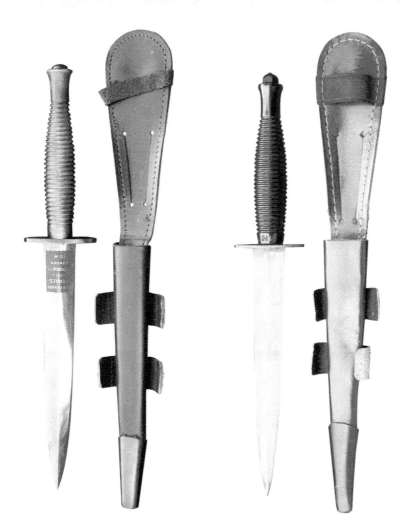

Ian Trenowden reports that when doing beach reconnaissance prior to D-Day, one COPPs swimmer lost his Commando dagger as well as the augers used to check the sand on the beach.[16] Their major worry was that the Germans would find the augers and realize a beach reconnaissance party had been ashore. Fortunately, a local Frenchman found one of the augers and hid it until the end of the war.

During an October 1942 raid on the island of Sark in the Channel Islands, members of the Small Scale Raiding Force managed to lose two F-S knives, which they left on the island. It may be supposed that the switch to the rubber retention band from the snap strap may have contributed to the loss of a substantial number of daggers over the course of the war.

In considering wartime use of the F-S and the US stilettos, it is worth remembering that for every incident related in memoirs or histories, there are likely to be dozens of others where the dagger performed its deadly mission but the details were never recorded. Many of those who used their Commando daggers to draw blood may never have related the story, though they are not likely to have forgotten it.

[16] Ian Trenowden, *Stealthily by Night*

THE COMMANDO DAGGER POSTWAR

Wilkinson and the British Commandos

After World War II, the Commando dagger remained in use around the world. Wilkinson continued to make the 3rd Pattern for military contracts and civilian sales, as well as special promotional daggers and commemorative models. The "Tom Beasley knife," produced by Wilkinson's master swordsmith of the same name, is perhaps the best known. Ironically, though this knife bears his name, Beasley may never have personally produced any F-S daggers. These very handsome daggers were actually manufactured as a promotional item for Wilkinson razors during the first years after the war. With an ivorine grip, gilt fittings, and etched blades, 500 of this model were produced. The "Beasley" knife has become quite sought after among collectors for its handsome appearance, but it does not have military provenance.

Robert Wilkinson-Latham estimates that Wilkinson produced about 10,000 further 3rd Pattern daggers in either black nickel or bright nickel finish between 1945 and 1970. These included private sale daggers and government orders. The author owns an interesting postwar Wilkinson Commando dagger from *c.*1952, marked with the Wilkinson logo on one side of the blade and the Army & Navy Store logo on the other. According to Robert Wilkinson-Latham, Wilkinson made these up in batches of six for the Army & Navy Stores, the cooperative which had originally been formed to supply Army and Navy officers with equipment and to ship items to postings all over the world. Postwar Wilkinson knives were normally designated as a "Commando knife" or "British fighting knife." The alloy handle was retained, though the pommel nut was replaced by a slotted one. Sheaths remained the same; in fact, Robert Wilkinson-Latham states that the company continued using up leftover World War II ones for decades, though they sometimes had to be re-stitched due to deterioration.

Throughout the postwar years there were purchases for the Royal Marine Commandos and for units assigned to the Commandos such as 29th Commando Regiment, Royal Artillery; Commando Helicopter Force; 59th Independent Commando Squadron, Royal Engineers; 131st Independent Commando Squadron, Royal Engineers (Territorial Army (TA)); and 289th Commando Battery, Royal Artillery (TA). One of the most interesting postwar orders for the Royal Marines arrived on May 18, 1982, for 250 daggers to be delivered in six days' time, destined for 3rd Commando Brigade in the Falklands. What is especially interesting is that the daggers were to be delivered to RAF Brize Norton, for onward shipment to 3rd Commando Brigade. Since the landings at San Carlos took place only three days after the placement of the order, on May 21, 1982, it is possible that the daggers were airdropped onto the beachhead. Wilkinson continued to fulfill government and private orders for Commando daggers until 2005. The Royal Navy and the British Army also appear to have ordered 3rd Pattern fighting knives from Wilkinson and possibly others during the postwar period.

Wilkinson also produced some nice commemorative knives in the World War II Victory Collection for the American Historical Foundation in 1980. One of the author's favorite postwar Wilkinson knives is a 3in S-Guard intended to resemble the earliest 1st Pattern knives. It is very handsome but the blade is unsharpened due to laws against double-edged blades in some places.

Various other Sheffield manufacturers produced 3rd Pattern daggers for individual sales and, in some cases, military contracts. J. Nowill & Sons made a substantial number. The author has seen J. Nowill knives in the possession of a couple of former members of the SAS, but does not know whether they were private purchase or unit purchase. H.G. Long produced postwar F-S-type knives, including some commemorative ones for the American Historical Foundation. Three Sheffield manufacturers produced Commando knives with NATO markings – Wilkinson Sword, John Clarke & Son, and George Ibberson. According to Ron Flook, some of these have been acquired for use in RAF survival kits. They are designated "knife, hunting GP with sheath W D pattern" and their NATO number is 5110-99-4658827.

Another interesting Wilkinson dagger which should be mentioned is the Army Air Corps helicopter escape knife, which was submitted to the British Army for evaluation in 2001. The handle was that of a full-sized 3rd Pattern Commando dagger, but the blade was only 3in long. The short blade was ground and tempered so that it could be used to punch through the helicopter's canopy for escape if the chopper went down. Although a couple of prototypes were submitted, the knife did not go into production.

The best-known users of the Commando dagger remain the Royal Marine Commandos, who view it as an important part of their heritage. In the recent conflict in Afghanistan, Royal Marine Commandos have been issued F-S daggers for the first time in nearly 30 years. The Commando dagger is still featured on the Royal Marines website in the section on weapons, and interestingly, on the website there is a short animated video showing the dagger being used by a Commando. What is noteworthy is that he draws the dagger from his support side (left side for a right-handed user) and demonstrates thrusts. Although most photos of World War II users seem to show the F-S carried on the strong side (right side for a right-hander) Fairbairn actually taught that it was best carried on the support side so that it could be presented with a sweeping slash when drawn. Various makers seem to have supplied daggers to the Royal Marines over the years since World War II, though those from Wilkinson have been highly valued by the Royal Marines known to the author.

An interesting though possibly apocryphal story was told to the author right after the Falklands War. While in Poole, Dorset, at the Old Harry (a pub popular at the time with members of the Special Boat Service), the author was having a pint with some friends just back from the Falklands. According to one of these, the Commandos had used their daggers once again in anger in the Falklands campaign, during the night fighting on Mount Kent and Mount Harriet. At the time, the author did not ask for details and he has not seen any corroboration for the report; however, the comments were made by a career Royal Marine.

Postwar Commando daggers exist with inscriptions for honor cadets at various British military colleges or for honor graduates of courses, which shows that the daggers were viewed as significant symbols of military excellence. Examples include a Queen's Cadet-Airborne dagger and one for a Marine Commando Cadet of the Year.

The postwar Commando dagger worldwide

Wilkinson's postwar production of Commando daggers was also sold to armed forces around the world. Postwar sales to foreign militaries included 400 to the Dutch in 1961 and 450 to the Norwegians in 1962 (both orders for black standard daggers), and between 1969 and 1979 there were orders of 250 for Ghana, 300 for Nigeria, and 500 for Kenya. In 1999, 125 were ordered for the Dutch Corps Commando Troepen. However, the German cutler Weyersberg, Kirschbaum, & Cie (WKC) purchased the Wilkinson tools in 2005 and now makes Commando knives. Linder, another German cutler, has offered an inexpensive copy of the Commando dagger. Other copies of the Commando dagger have been produced in various parts of the world.

Many of the postwar units which have used the Commando dagger are descendants of the World War II Commandos or SAS. As the World War II Free French 1st Parachute Chausseur Regiment, Commandos, and SAS formed the basis for French airborne, Commando, and other special forces troops who would fight in Indochina and Algeria, many took their Commando daggers with them into the postwar French forces. For others joining those units, the award of a Commando dagger upon graduation from training became the sign of elite status.

The Commando dagger issued to Indonesia's Kopassus special forces unit carries the unit's badge on blade and sheath. Note the same badge on the unit's maroon beret and also that the badge incorporates a Commando dagger.

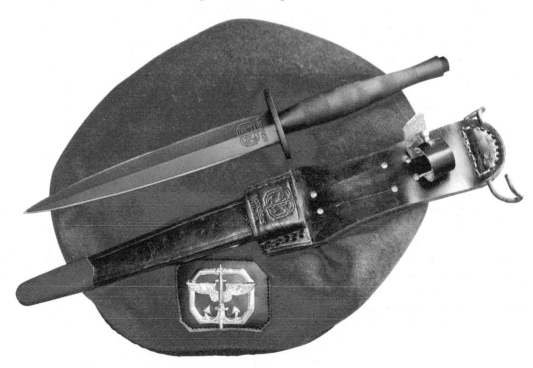

The green arm-sheath and green-handled 3rd Pattern Commando dagger marked "PPCLI" (Princess Patricia's Canadian Light Infantry) and reportedly used when the "Princess Pats" were assigned the airborne role.

Versions of the dagger marked "Commando" have been produced in France and used by French airborne, Commando, Legion, and other elite troops. The French also made a prototype submachine gun bayonet based on the F-S design. These knives have a diamond-shaped crossguard and are heavier than postwar Sheffield Commando daggers. The sheath on this French version also has a metal reinforcing strip on the back.

One of the most interesting French versions of the F-S is the 1953 "COMMANDO" dagger. It is said that this dagger was originally created by a member of the 11th Shock Parachute Regiment and used by various French special forces units during the Indochina and Algeria counterinsurgency campaigns between 1954 and 1962. The blade is double-edged and about 6½in long. Crossguards are normally marked "LE COMMANDO INOX" and "MARQUES & MODELES DEPOSES/SUPER-NOGENT."

Reportedly, too, versions of the dagger have been produced in Spain for Spanish airborne troops. An Indonesian copy has been supplied for elite Indonesian military units. Malaysian special forces use a version of the Commando dagger, possibly produced in Indonesia and marked with Malaysian unit markings. Singapore also issues an F-S-style dagger to its Commandos. According to one of the author's sources, the first knives ordered for the Indonesian Kopassus (special forces) were made in Germany, then copied in Indonesia. Other very cheap copies have been made in the Far East.

The Commando daggers issued to Singapore's Commandos, Malaysia's Grup Gerak Khas, Indonesia's Kopassus, and Indonesia's Jala Menkara (Marine Corps) are all marked with the unit's insignia and are generally presented when an operator has completed selection and training. However, it appears that the daggers are not considered just ceremonial but are carried as operational weapons with at least some of the units.

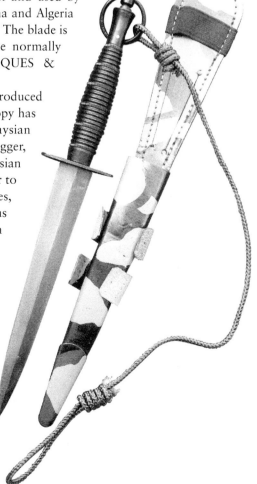

One of the 3rd Pattern-type Commando daggers made in Australia and carrying "SPEARMAN" and "SEATO" markings on the handguard. Note the distinctive large ring through the pommel.

Though not really postwar production knives, knives often encountered by US collectors with "ENGLAND" stamped on the crossguard were surplus purchased from the British government in 1947 and imported into the USA for sale. Although normally these knives are of the 3rd Pattern, 1st and 2nd Pattern knives are believed to have been imported as well. The total number of knives in this surplus purchase has been cited as 167,000.

As mentioned previously, a blackened version of the USMC stiletto was reportedly issued to Canadian airborne troops during World War II and possibly continued in use after the war. There are also what some called the "Canadian parachutist's Commando dagger" or "Princess Patricia's Canadian Light Infantry knife." The author had an example of this knife which was a 3rd Pattern with the handle green and with PPCLI and a Canadian broad arrow C acceptance mark. The knives may have been manufactured by William Rodgers in the early years after the war as the PPCLI had an airborne role during the post-World War II/Korean War era. The author's example had a green arm/calf sheath which was marked "KNIFE, PARACHUTIST/SLEEVE-SCABBARD, MK 1/H. SHEFFIELD, M.45." The broad arrow C mark was also on the sheath. The author has owned one of the arm sheathes obtained from a World War II special forces soldier who purchased it late in the war and used it with an F-S on the calf. He has also owned a second example of these daggers in a sheath obtained from Canada; that sheath was not green, though the knife had the green handle. The author has not been able to obtain confirmation from any veterans of the PPCLI during the period that they used the arm sheath.

There were also presentation F-S-type knives produced on Okinawa for the 46th Special Forces Company (Airborne) assigned to Thailand during the Vietnam War or for members of the 5th Special Forces Group (Airborne) who had served in Vietnam.

In addition, there was a postwar Australian F-S type knife marked "SEATO No/ 295341/70" and "SPEARMAN" on the handguard, which was used by Australian troops during the Vietnam War. The handle is of 3rd Pattern type, but with a pattern similar to the "ribbed and beaded" handles made during World War II. However, instead of beads it uses ridged bands. The knife is normally blackened and the examples the author has seen have an oversized ring through the handle and a sheath in camouflage colors. A New Zealand 3rd Pattern knife exists as well with a brass hilt affixed to the tang without a pommel nut.

As this is written, in 2010, it is almost certain that special operations troops deployed in various parts of the world have a Commando dagger about their persons. The classic F-S stiletto design remains beloved by elite troops; even though they realize its design faults, its link to their "Commando" heritage generally trumps any flaws.

IMPACT
The icon of special forces

The influence of the F-S dagger has resulted in the fighting knife holding an important place in the mythology and the training of many elite military units. Part of special forces training today is instilling a willingness to close with the enemy and eliminate him at close quarters with whichever weapon is most effective. Often, this is the fighting knife and, surprisingly often, still the F-S dagger.

The basic design of the Fairbairn-Sykes fighting knife remains popular today and reproductions of varying quality may be found from many sources. One market for the myriad copies of the 3rd Pattern is re-enactors who "interpret" World War II Commandos, Rangers, or paratroopers and carry a Commando knife as part of their gear. A Commando dagger on the belt or affixed to battle dress lends a sense of authenticity and adds to the martial air of the combat troops they try to recreate. And, just as they did when they first saw Commandos and their daggers in the 1940s, many boys and a few girls feel a thrill and a realization that even today, in the era of stealth aircraft, Predator drones, and precision-guided munitions, there still remain combat situations when cold steel is the final arbiter – the ultimate precision-guided weapon if you will!

One of the most obvious influences of the Fairbairn-Sykes dagger is its symbolism among elite military units. The US Ranger Memorial features a giant Commando dagger as a key design element. British, US, Australian, French, Dutch, Belgian, and other special forces units with links to the Commandos, SAS, etc often present a framed or inscribed Commando dagger to commemorate special occasions or accomplishments. Countries such as Malaysia and Singapore with former colonial ties to British Commandos and special forces – as well as Indonesia with its ties to American, Dutch, and Australian special forces – award daggers bearing the unit's insignia to their personnel upon completion of their selection and training process. Many other countries have a special knife awarded upon completion of airborne or special forces training. Sometimes the knife is based on the F-S and sometimes it is a totally local design, but the tradition was often started after a training exchange when an operator brought home a presentation Commando dagger.

The Fairbairn-Sykes has had a profound influence on the insignia of world commando and special forces units. The first units to incorporate the F-S dagger into their insignia were part of the Special Service Brigade, formed in October 1940 from the Independent Companies and the early Commandos. The Special Service Brigade HQ had an interesting insignia that incorporated two F-S knives with the red "SS" for Special Service forming the S-guards of the knives. The brigade signals unit had an

A patrol of L Detachment, SAS, just back from a desert mission; the Arab headdress was adopted from the Long Range Desert Group. Note that the officer in the foreground carries his 1st Pattern F-S dagger. (IWM E21337)

insignia incorporating a lightning bolt crossed with an F-S dagger. 2 Commando used an F-S on its cap badge and shoulder insignia. French Marine Commandos used a shield with the Cross of Lorraine, a sailing ship, and a Commando dagger for their beret badge; this beret badge is still worn by French Marine Commandos. 5 Commando used a Roman numeral V between crossed F-S daggers. By late in the war, Royal Marine Commandos were wearing a triangular shoulder insignia with an F-S, point up. The current Royal Marine Commando shoulder insignia retains this basic design. V Force, which operated in India and later Burma, used crossed F-S daggers with a "V" superimposed. The World War II Canadian Parachute Battalion had officers' collar insignia which incorporated an F-S in a hand coming from a cloud. Although it is often mistakenly stated that the SAS cap badge incorporates an F-S dagger, this does not appear be the case. Instead, the blade is supposed to be Excalibur.

In the postwar years, even more units have used the F-S in their insignia. In addition to the British and French Marine Commandos who have continued to wear their same basic insignia since the war, postwar units which have used the F-S dagger or a similar dagger on their insignia include: Canadian Special Service Force, Australian Commandos, Belgian Paracommandos, some French airborne units, Zaire Commandos, Republic of Vietnam Rangers, Republic of Vietnam Provincial Recon Units, Republic of South Africa Recce, Indonesian Kopassus, and Afghanistan airborne forces. Ironically, even West Germany had Kampfschwimmer insignia which bore a blade that looked much like an F-S. Various US units have used the F-S or the US World War II equivalents on their insignia. Some US airborne insignia has borne the F-S, while myriad US Special Forces insignia have borne the V-42 dagger since the special forces are deemed descendants of the 1st Special Service Force as well as the OSS Operational Groups. US Marine Recon units and MARSOC (Marine Special Forces assigned to Special Operations Command) have used the Raider stiletto on their insignia, though often the blade appears to be a generic F-S dagger. There are many more which could be listed, but the point that the F-S is a key element of elite unit symbolism should be obvious.

At least one US World War II version of the F-S saw more than symbolic usage during the April 1961 Bay of Pigs invasion, when CIA operatives working with the Cuban exiles issued out most or all of the OSS stilettos remaining in stores. Some US advisors kept one or more for themselves and all appear in mint unused condition, though the rubber washers have deteriorated in some cases.

MODERN FIGHTING KNIVES

Because the 1st Pattern F-S dagger is such a classic design various custom knifemakers have attempted to reproduce it. The author considers the best of these salutes to the original F-S to be those from Peter Parkinson in New Zealand.

Parkinson Custom Fairbairn-Sykes 1st Pattern knives

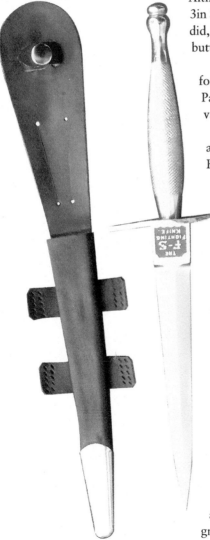

An example of the beautiful custom reproduction F-S daggers produced by Peter Parkinson of New Zealand. Although he uses a wartime "F-S Fighting Knife" logo, on the reverse of the ricasso he previously used his own feather marking but has now created a Parkinson logo similar to the original Wilkinson logo in appearance.

Peter Parkinson has attempted to recreate early Fairbairn-Sykes knives with great craftsmanship. His 1st Pattern knife is of 440C hand-ground carbon steel which is heat treated, then hand polished. Although on one side of the ricasso he uses the F-S Fighting Knife logo, on the reverse he uses his own logo instead of that of Wilkinson Sword. As a result, it is obviously a custom reproduction, though an extremely fine one. As with original F-S daggers, the handle is of brass stock which is diamond knurled, then nickel plated. Parkinson uses a sheath with a snap retention strap and tabs of brown leather with a nickel chape; this is correct for a 1st Pattern knife. Parkinson also makes a nickel or black 2nd Pattern F-S which does not have any logo.

A very interesting reproduction which Parkinson no longer makes is what he termed the "X dagger" based on the early pre-F-S knife reportedly made from surplus bayonets and having a 7½in needlepoint blade. Although the originals of this type of knife normally had a 3in S-guard, Parkinson used a 2nd Pattern-type guard on his. He did, however, supply the "Camp X"-style sheath designed to be buttoned inside the waistband of the trousers.

Parkinson had problems getting the brass for his handles for some months and so began making very handsome 1st Pattern-type knives with handles of other materials, including various woods and what appears to be ivory polymer.

In addition to the reproduction knives, there have also been various attempts to improve upon the original Fairbairn-Sykes design, in at least one case with Fairbairn's involvement. Three of the most interesting of these attempts are discussed below.

The Randall fighting stiletto

Many US troops encountered the Fairbairn-Sykes during World War II and wanted a knife with similar characteristics, but also designed to hold up to extremely hard usage. The custom Randall fighting stiletto, which came to be known as the Randall Model 2, was introduced in April 1943, and was designed to meet the needs of US troops wanting a stiletto fighting knife. Fabricated of high-quality ¼in-thick steel, the Model 2 had a wide stiletto blade with a sturdy point that would resist breakage. Typical blade length was 7in, but since the Model 2 was a custom-made knife, troops could order other lengths. For example, World War II Model 2s with a 1½in-wide, 8in-long blade are known. The weight of this big Model 2 is 13oz. In some ways, fighting techniques with this knife might be more akin to those used with a Smatchet than with the elegant F-S. At least a few Model 2 fighting stilettos were made with a blood groove in the blade.

The stacked leather washer handle helped orient the knife correctly and gave a very sure grip. Model 2 stilettos had a brass crossguard and a Duraluminum pommel cap with a lanyard hole. The sturdy leather sheaths incorporated a pocket for a sharpening stone, a feature much admired by troops as they could sharpen their Randall whenever it was convenient.

Troops liked the fact that the Model 2 served as an excellent close combat knife yet could still perform utility chores such as prying without breaking. The Model 2 proved equally popular with troops in Korea and Vietnam. In Vietnam, many US Ranger advisors to the BDQ (Vietnamese Rangers) carried Model 2 Randalls. The Model 2 is still made today and is very popular with special operations troops who have carried it during the War on Terror.

The author agrees; he has used a Model 2 for more than 25 years, often on contract training or security jobs when it has served as a close combat knife and occasionally as a utility knife. Recently, he acquired a Model 2 in an upside-down shoulder holster, which was made by Randall in very limited numbers. Though the Randall is relatively large it carries fairly well, and this set-up also has a degree of historical appeal since some original Shanghai knives were carried in shoulder rigs.

Randall fighting stiletto shown next to a 1st Pattern F-S dagger. The fighting stiletto was designed for US troops who had seen the Fairbairn-Sykes dagger but wanted a sturdier knife incorporating some of its features. Randall still makes this design today.

The Applegate-Fairbairn dagger

Fairly early in World War II, the faults of the F-S dagger became apparent to those who used it in combat and to the instructors who taught its use. Although some early aspects of the design of the Applegate-Fairbairn knife are open to discussion, Rex Applegate has told the author that, while serving together training OSS agents, he and Fairbairn discussed improvements to the

A version of the Applegate-Fairbairn knife designed to correct the "deficiencies" in the F-S dagger. Note the shorter, wider blade, ribbed handle, and reproduction signatures of Applegate and Fairbairn.

67

F-S dagger. Sketches were made, and while serving at the Military Intelligence School at Camp Ritchie, MD, in late 1944 or early 1945, Applegate had a prototype made in the machine shop. Applegate also had "Bo" Randall of Randall Made Knives produce a number (the generally accepted figure is 11) of prototype knives with some features similar to the A-F during 1944.

Some experts feel that Fairbairn had little actual input on the A-F dagger and that his own improvement on the F-S was the "Cobra" knife developed when he was training the Cyprus Police in 1956. Based on a photograph posted with an online article by Fairbairn authority W.L. Cassidy, the Cobra had a curved claw-like blade with some similarities to "raptor" blades favored by some today.

In the 1970s, Applegate decided to put the Applegate-Fairbairn knife into production. Applegate had various well-known knifemakers make prototypes or small production runs during the evolution of the A-F. Among those who made these early versions were T.J. Yancy, Bo Loveless, Barry Wood, Bill Harsey, and Al Mar.

In 1993, Applegate licensed BlackJack Knives to produce the Applegate-Fairbairn dagger. As produced by BlackJack, the A-F had a double-edged 6¼in blade with central rib which was broader than the F-S and had a point much less likely to break. Blade thickness was ³⁄₁₆in, and most BlackJack blades were of 440A steel but some were in A2. Rockwell hardness was 56–58. The crossguard was of brass and was curved slightly downward. The handles were of Lexan with longitudinal ribs and incorporated a lanyard hole. An interesting feature was a series of weights under the grips which could be adjusted to give the wielder the proper balance to fit his own tastes. Many preferred the hilt-heavy feel of the original F-S. Overall length was 11¼in. The standard BlackJack sheath was of leather with a velcro retention strap, though nylon sheaths were also offered at some point during production.

As a result of disagreements over royalties between Applegate and BlackJack, production of the BlackJack versions of the A-F was terminated after approximately 7,000 had been produced. Eventually, the German knifemaker Boker began producing Applegate-Fairbairn knives and continues to make examples today.

The UK-SFK

UK-SFK stands for "United Kingdom Special Forces Knife." Manufactured by BlackHawk Products Group, the UK-SFK is designed to offer a contemporary fighting knife for the SAS and SBS (and it is possibly also in use with other units). Although the F-S remained in use with British airborne troops, Commandos, and special forces for decades after World War II, the UK-SFK is viewed as an improvement over the original F-S, but an improvement that retains some of the traditional F-S features. Designed by Michael Janich, who had substantial contact with Applegate before his death and is well aware of the traditional F-S, the Applegate-Fairbairn, and other knife designs, the UK-SFK retains the balance of the F-S and its liveliness in the hand.

As does virtually any knife designed to improve on the original F-S design, the UK-SFK has a thicker and stronger D-2 Tool Steel spear-point blade, though the double-edged "stiletto" profile is retained to some extent. The handle is flat, with finger grooves for orientation, and it is well designed to not turn in the hand. G-10 scales help the user to grip the knife securely even with wet hands. Despite the F-S influences, the UK-SFK incorporates features from other blades. For example the influence of knifemaker and designer Brent Beshara shows in the integral crossguard and in the flat handle. The hilt tapers into a flat which may be used as a skull crusher or window breaker and incorporates a lanyard hole. Black, epoxy powder coat or brushed satin blades are available.

The sheath and mounting system incorporate features specifically requested in the bid specifications from the special forces units involved. Of injection-molded nylon, the sheath's retention system incorporates BlackHawk's Serpa technology as a release button is depressed naturally as the knife is drawn. Designed to be mounted to a combat vest using MOLLE (modular lightweight load-carrying equipment) gear, the sheath comes with various mounting plates, screws, and washers. Using either long or short plates, the sheath may be mounted for knife presentation with the handle up, down, or across the chest. It may also be mounted as a drop sheath for wear on the thigh. The author has carried a UK-SFK mounted upside-down on his assault vest for months now and found that the mounting and retention systems work extremely well.

The UK-SFK is well designed as a close combat knife with a handle that lends itself to fencing or ice pick grips and to various fighting techniques. Due to the pronounced finger grooves on the handle, the UK-SFK works quite well when wearing tactical gloves, too. Though intended not for utility use but as a combat knife, the UK-SFK is tough enough to stand up to bush chores. The UK-SFK is stylish and has panache. It is a suitable knife for the descendants of the units which first used the Fairbairn-Sykes dagger.

The UK-SFK (United Kingdom-Special Forces Knife) being produced for British special forces units is the first new combat knife for the units since World War II. It incorporates some F-S features but uses a very modern sheath which may be carried in myriad ways.

CONCLUSION

Winston Churchill strongly believed in the concept of the Commandos both as an actual force to disrupt the German occupation of Europe and as a double-edged psychological weapon, which would not only give the British people military successes at a dark time and keep the spirit of attack alive, but would also shake German confidence and complacency. About the Commandos, Churchill said, "There comes out from the sea from time to time a hand of steel which plucks the German sentries with growing efficiency." The steel in that "hand" was the Fairbairn-Sykes Commando dagger.

In 1942, Gordon Holman, the war correspondent for the Exchange Telegraph Company, wrote one of the first books on the Commandos, *Commando Attack*. The book was meant to give the British public a look at the men who were pricking the German defenses with raids, keeping Britain's attacking spirit alive until it and the Allies were ready to go on a broader offensive. He used the Fairbairn-Sykes dagger to illustrate the deadly effectiveness of the Commandos:

> It is true, too, that the Commandos know all about the use of knives – not in the approved film-villain fashion, but scientifically, with wrist-work playing an important part and little more than an inch of the stiletto-like blade needed to kill a man. These Commando knives are strong, all-metal weapons with a blade about six inches long. They mostly carry them slipped into a slit-pocket in the leg of their trousers so that their hand is always near the hilt. It is curious that in these days, when so many high-grade weapons have been perfected for killing at close range or otherwise, cold steel, one of the oldest weapons, should remain so menacing. I hope I never have to make the choice but I think I would rather meet a Commando soldier with a Tommy gun than with one of those knives!

Quite likely today, most would rather meet a special forces soldier with a firearm than one with a knife. Knives are messy and bloody and leave gaping wounds. Whether a Fairbairn-Sykes dagger or one of its descendants, a fighting knife gives the elite fighter a sense of his own competence and ability to inflict death and destruction without high-tech weaponry. In fact, well-trained special forces troops realize that within a certain distance – 20ft or less – an operator with a blade may well have the advantage over an enemy with a gun. In the dark with surprise on his side, the balance tips even more to favor the blade.

Fairbairn and Sykes were well aware of the advantages of the knife in certain deadly encounters. They were also aware that they needed to take a lot of young men raised to be law-abiding and God-fearing and turn them into killers quickly. Training in hand-to-hand combat and with the blade helped them accomplish this. The Fairbairn-Sykes gave the newly minted Commandos and other troops the tool to kill the enemy up close in the dark, but it also gave them a symbol of their own elite status – they were trained to use cold steel to a high degree of lethality, and just like their daggers they were tempered and sharpened. For many months, the Commandos were the "stiletto" point of the British armed forces delivering thrusts against the exposed belly of the Axis. The "stiletto" points of their F-S daggers were a constant reminder of that mission.

The term "iconic" may be overused today but few would deny that the Fairbairn-Sykes is an iconic weapon. It has a cold and deadly look, yet it is stylish – almost elegant, much as some predators among animals are deadly yet beautiful at the same time. Collectors love the F-S and other Commando daggers because they are emotive of some of the best fighting men the world has ever seen. Many elite military units still like the Commando dagger, either as a combat knife or as a symbol, because it offers a link to their history and reminds them that their job in wartime still comes down to delivering a killing stroke to their enemy. Some martial artists who practice blade techniques still like the F-S design for its balance and swiftness in the hand.

Though a 70-year-old design, the Fairbairn-Sykes dagger is probably the most widely recognized combat knife in the world. A few may still call it a Fairbairn-Sykes dagger; far more are likely to call it a Commando dagger or Commando knife; some will call it a military fighting knife. Whatever they call it, they will recognize the knife, its history and its purpose.

APPENDIX

Units that used the Fairbairn-Sykes dagger during World War II

Special Service Brigade

The first Commando organization, established 1940, which by March 1941 would have 11 commandos under its direction. It was replaced in October 1943 by Special Service Group. The first Fairbairn-Sykes knives were made to fulfill orders for units under the Special Service Brigade.

Special Service Group

The parent organization for the remainder of World War II until all remaining Commandos became part of the Royal Marines in 1946.

1st Special Service/1st Commando Brigade

Formed for the Normandy invasion and landed on June 6, 1944, the 1st SSB fought in France until September 7, 1944, when it returned to the UK to prepare for deployment to the Far East. The brigade returned to Europe in January 1945 after the Ardennes offensive and served there for the remainder of the war, often being used to secure bridges during the advance into Germany.

2nd Special Service/2nd Commando Brigade

Formed in Italy in November 1943, 2nd SSB was used for various operations in the Adriatic, and took part in other operations in Italy including the Anzio landings. Later, elements of 2nd SSB carried out mountain assaults during the advance in Italy, while other elements returned to Anzio to carry out raids against German positions. Portions of the brigade worked with Yugoslav partisans against German-held islands. The brigade fought in Italy until the German surrender there and remained on occupation duty until postwar.

3rd Special Service/3rd Commando Brigade

Formed in November 1943 for operations in Southeast Asia, some elements of 3rd SSB saw action in Burma. Later, the brigade was withdrawn to India to prepare for operations in Malaya, but the Japanese surrender caused cancellation. Postwar, 40, 42, and 45 Royal Marine Commandos were in this brigade and would form the basis for the modern Commandos, RM.

4th Special Service/4th Commando Brigade

This unit was formed in summer 1943 of Royal Marine Commandos for the Normandy landings. During the Allied advance out of Normandy and into Germany, 4th SSB helped capture bridges, carried out night raids, and worked with Resistance fighters. Although scheduled for deployment to the Far East after VE Day, 4th SSB was not needed once the Japanese surrendered and was disbanded in 1946.

1 Commando

This unit took part in early Commando raids including Pointe de Saire. Later 1 Commando took part in the *Torch* landings in North Africa in November 1942. In 1943, 1 Commando joined 3rd Commando Brigade for operations in the Far East where it remained until war's end. Members of 1 Commando had volunteered to form the basis of British airborne forces early in the war.

2 Commando

This commando was originally intended as an airborne unit but was later trained for amphibious operations. In December 1941, elements of 2 Commando took part in the Vaagso raid. Later, 2 Commando took part in landings on Sicily, fought with the Yugoslav partisans, and ended the war in combat against the Germans in Italy.

3 Commando

This unit took part in some of the best known of the early Commando raids including those against Guernsey and Dieppe. In February 1943, 3 Commando was sent to Gibraltar to be available for raids against Spain should it enter the war on the German side. 3 Commando took part in landings on Sicily and the toe of Italy, then returned to the UK to prepare for the Normandy landings. As part of 1st SSB, 3 Commando took part in the landings on June 6, 1944, then in advances across Germany, including the Rhine crossings and an attack on a V2 rocket factory.

4 Commando

Elements of 4 Commando were on the Vaagso raid, and the commando also took part in the Dieppe raid. Assigned to eliminate a German battery, 4 Commando landed on June 6, 1944, on the Normandy beachhead. The commando joined 4th SSB for the Walcheren assault and other operations in the Scheldt Estuary.

5 Commando

Formed in July 1940, many of the troops incorporated into 5 Commando had escaped from Dunkirk. Members of the Commando took part in the St Nazaire raid. Later, 5 Commando landed on the island of Madagascar to capture it from Vichy French forces. Serving in 3rd SSB, 5 Commando took part in operations in Southeast Asia.

6 Commando

Although formed in the summer of 1940 and used in abortive raids on islands in the Atlantic, 6 Commando first saw major action during the *Torch* landings in North Africa of November 8, 1942. The commando operated in North Africa until April 1943, when it returned to the UK to prepare for the Normandy landings. After landing on June 6, 1944, 6 Commando advanced to reinforce airborne troops holding bridges over the Caen Canal and Orne River bridges. Later, 6 Commando took part in the combat crossing of the Rhine at Wesel on March 23/24, 1945, then took part in the crossing of the Weser on April 7/8. The final river crossing of the war for 6 Commando was the Elbe on April 29.

7 Commando

This commando was formed in August 1940. After arriving in Egypt in March 1940, members of the commando took part in a raid on Bardia in April. Committed to action during the defense of

Crete on May 27–31, 1941, many members of 7 Commando were captured fighting a rearguard action during the withdrawal. As a result, 7 Commando was disbanded with remaining members joining Middle East Commando.

8 Commando

Formed in June 1940, 8 Commando was also deployed to Egypt where it was used in the rearguard actions on Crete and later in an attack near Tobruk. The unit was disbanded in July 1941.

9 Commando

Formed in summer 1940, 9 Commando was originally trained for raids along the French coast but was deployed to Gibraltar then used for operations against islands in the Adriatic. On January 22, 1944, 9 Commando landed at Anzio but within a week was withdrawn to take part in the mountain advance up Italy's spine. The commando returned to Anzio in March to take part in patrols against German positions. In May 1944, a troop of 9 Commando rescued PoWs from behind German lines. Later in 1944, 9 Commando joined with elements of the Greek Sacred Squadron to operate against the Germans on Greek islands and later mainland Greece. They took part in the liberation of Athens, then returned to Italy in February 1945, in time for action around Lake Comacchio in April.

The men of 3 Commando were in action from the Dieppe raid to the Rhine crossings – with daggers to hand, if not always in their teeth. (IWM H19284)

A member of the Free French forces serving in 10 (Inter-Allied) Commando sharpens his Commando dagger. (IWM H38951)

operations in Norway, as did Czech Commandos in Czechoslovakia. X Troop carried out raids behind German lines, often to disrupt German communications, and also infiltrated through the lines using their language ability. In many cases, small groups from 10 Commando served with other units providing translators who could fight on the front lines. They also carried out many small classified raids. After the war, members of 10 Commando provided the basis for the special forces units of the newly liberated countries.

11 Commando

Formed in late 1940, 11 Commando was often known as Scottish Commando. Sent to the Middle East, 11 Commando landed against the French in Syria in June 1941, suffering heavy casualties. The unit was withdrawn to Cyprus and disbanded, many members joining Middle East Commando.

12 Commando

Often known as the Irish and Welsh Commando, 12 Commando was formed in 1941 from men from Northern Ireland and the Welsh regiments. Members of 12 Commando augmented by Norwegian troops took part in the Lofoten Islands raid during December, 1942. Commandos from 12 Commando took part in other raids during 1943, many against targets in Norway.

14 Commando

This Commando was raised in 1943 and trained for Arctic warfare, possibly for raids against German bases in Norway, before being disbanded the same year. Canadians were recruited for this unit. Its mission appears similar to that envisioned for the 1st Special Service Force discussed below.

30 Commando

Also known as the Special Engineering Unit and 30th Assault Unit, 30 Commando was formed in the summer of 1941, with Ian Fleming of "Bond, James Bond" fame being involved in its formation and operations. The primary mission of the unit was the capture of German technology, scientific papers, etc. Members were also involved in the hunt for German scientists. Operations continued until late 1945.

10 (Inter-Allied) Commando

The Inter-Allied Commando was formed in January 1942, with an original basis of French Marines and Dutch Army. It would eventually incorporate personnel from other occupied countries including Poland, Norway, and Belgium. German-speaking troops from Germany, Austria, Denmark, Hungary, Yugoslavia, Czechoslovakia, Rumania, as well as Alsace-Lorraine, formed X Troop. French Commandos from 10 Commando took part in the Dieppe raid, then later landed on D-Day with 4 Commando. Later, French Commandos worked with the Resistance, took part in the advance towards Paris, and near the end of the war took part in operations around the Scheldt Estuary. Dutch Commandos took part in the landing at Westkappelle in November 1944, and carried out other raids. Belgian and Polish Commandos served in Italy and later Yugoslavia with 2nd SSB and were known for aggressive patrolling in the Apennines. Norwegian Commandos from 10 Commando carried out raids and intelligence

Middle East Commando

This commando unit was attached to the Eighth Army in North Africa and is best known for the November 1941 mission against Rommel's headquarters. Early in 1942 Middle East Commando was disbanded. The unit is often associated with a special knuckle-duster fighting knife.

Chindits

Under Orde Wingate, the Chindits carried out long-term operations and raids behind Japanese lines during 1943 and 1944.

Royal Marine Commandos

40 (RM) Commando was raised in February 1942, took part in the Dieppe landings, and later fought in Italy and the Adriatic.

41 (RM) Commando took part in landings in Sicily, Salerno, Normandy, and Walcheren.

42 (RM) Commando served in Burma during 1944–45.

43 (RM) Commando took part in the January 1944 Anzio landings, then fought in the Adriatic and Italy for the remainder of the war.

44 (RM) Commando took part in operations in Burma during 1944–45.

45 (RM) Commando landed on June 6, 1944, as part of the Normandy invasion and took part in the drive into Germany.

46 (RM) Commando landed in Normandy, then was used for river crossings during the advance into Germany.

47 (RM) Commando landed in Normandy on June 6, 1944, and later saw action during the Walcheren landings.

48 (RM) Commando landed in Normandy on June 6, 1944 and later took part in the Walcheren landings.

The tradition of the World War II Commandos continues today in 40, 42, and 45 Royal Marine Commandos, which in the postwar years consolidated the other RM Commando units.

Special Air Service (SAS)

The 1st SAS was formed in February 1943, under LtCol David Stirling as a raiding unit to operate behind German lines in North Africa, primarily against Luftwaffe airfields. 2nd SAS was formed primarily for service among the Greek islands where it was known as the 1st Raiding Squadron. After Stirling's capture by the Germans, 1st SAS was commanded by the legendary LtCol "Paddy" Mayne, who was the top "ace" in the war in North Africa having destroyed so many German aircraft on raids. Later in the war, SAS patrols parachuted into occupied Europe to work with partisans, especially during the weeks before D-Day. In January 1944, there were five SAS regiments, of which two were British, two were French, and one was Belgian. Of course, in the postwar years, the British SAS would become one of the world's most respected special forces units.

SAS patrol commander Lt Edward McDonald wears his F-S dagger during the unit's time in the Western Desert. Standing and talking with McDonald is David Stirling, founder of the SAS. (IWM E21339)

Special Boat Section

Initially formed from a Folbot Troop assigned to Layforce in the Middle East and later assigned to 1st SAS, the unit originally formed D Squadron, and later the Special Boat Squadron which operated throughout the Aegean. In 1943, another "Special Boat Section" was formed as part of the Commandos and designated 2nd SBS. The Special Boat Squadron of 1st SAS eventually expanded to regimental status. Because the titles "Special Boat Section" and "Special Boat Squadron" were both used during the war, this has created a lot of confusion over the years, especially since the current descendant of these units is the "Special Boat Service." Sometimes designated Special Boat Sections were raiding units in the Far East that used small boats. Far Eastern units often operated under Small Operations Group (SOG). Today's Royal Marine Special Boat Service, Britain's naval special ops units, is descended from the wartime SBS units.

Combined Operations Assault Pilotage Parties (COPPs)

COPPs operatives were swimmers and canoeists who specialized in carrying out clandestine hydrographic surveys of beaches prior to the Allied landings in France, Sicily, Italy, Greece, Malaya, and Sumatra, as well as recces for the Rhine crossings. Because of the nature of their operations which entailed infiltrating onto enemy beaches, COPPs members reportedly relied heavily on edged weapons such as the F-S. Today's SBS has absorbed the COPPs mission.

Royal Marines Boom Patrol Detachment

Another raiding detachment which used canoes, this unit is best known for the "Cockleshell Heroes" raid against shipping in Bordeaux Harbor during December 1942. Later, members of the Boom Patrol Detachment operated in the Mediterranean infiltrating harbors and placing limpet mines. This unit is considered another forerunner of today's SBS.

Sea Reconnaissance Unit (SRU)

The SRU was formed for the purpose of carrying out long-distance recon missions using paddle boards and/or scuba gear. Particularly strong swimmers were recruited. In actuality, the unit's primary employment seems to have been recceing for river crossings in Burma.

Royal Navy Beach Commandos

The Beach Commandos came in early to coordinate operations on beachheads during Allied landings. Beach Commandos attended the Commando course at Achnacarry as well as specialized Royal Naval training. Organized into company-sized units, the Beach Commandos went ashore with the first elements of assault troops to keep troops and supplies flowing off the beachhead. Often, the Naval Commandos operated under heavy fire, helping to evacuate the wounded and taking charge of PoWs in addition to other duties. From early 1942 until the end of the war the RN Commandos were involved in every major landing.

British Airborne Forces (Parachute Regiment)

Originally formed in June 1940, after Winston Churchill called for a unit with the capabilities of the German *Fallschirmjäger* which had carried out lightning strikes in Holland and Belgium, by the end of World War II British airborne forces would comprise 17 battalions serving in the 1st Airborne Division, 6th Airborne Division, and 2nd Parachute Brigade. Additionally,

Members of the Home Guard (possibly members of "last ditch" stay-behind parties) receive training in use of the Commando dagger for carotid thrusts at the Commando Training Centre at Achnacarry. Such high-level training was not the norm for Home Guard units. (IWM H31546)

there were the 50th and 77th Indian parachute brigades. Major jumps carried out by British airborne troops included: Operations *Husky* (Sicily), *Overlord* (Normandy), *Dragoon* (southern France), *Market Garden* (Arnhem), and *Varsity* (Rhine crossing).

US Marine Raiders

The Marine Raiders were one of two US units to be formed with missions similar to the Commandos. The 1st and 2nd Marine Raider battalions were formed in February 1942, followed by the 3rd Raider Battalion in September 1942, and the 4th Raider Battalion in October 1942. The 1st Raider Battalion is best remembered for its operations on Guadalcanal and later heavy fighting on New Georgia. The 2nd Raider Battalion took part in a raid on Makin Atoll in August 1942, then in November 1942 raided behind Japanese lines on Guadalcanal. In November 1943, the 2nd Raider Battalion landed on Bougainville where it fought until withdrawn in January 1944. The 3rd Marine Raider Battalion first saw action in February 1944, when it carried out a diversionary raid to cover a US Army landing in the Russell Islands. The unit later fought on Bougainville. The 4th Raider Battalion first saw action on New Georgia where it was used for raids and recon patrols. At times, the Paramarines operated with the Raider battalions. All four Raider battalions were disbanded in January/February 1944.

US Army Rangers

Before the end of World War II, there would be six Ranger battalions. The 1st Ranger Battalion was formed in June 1942, and at times was known as "Darby's Rangers" after its first commanding officer, LtCol William O. Darby. The 1st Rangers trained with the Commandos and at least some went on early Commando raids, including the one at Dieppe. The 1st Rangers took part in the D-Day landings, the Salerno landings, and the Anzio landings. A typical Ranger mission (and a typical Commando mission, as well) was destroying artillery emplacements which could fire on Allied landing craft. During fighting in Italy, the 1st Battalion was virtually destroyed. The 2nd Ranger Battalion was formed in the USA in April

1943, and saw heavy action after landing at Pointe du Hoc on D-Day. The 2nd Battalion operated on the flank of the US 29th Division during the attack on Brest. Next, the 2nd Rangers moved east, seeing combat in the Huertgen Forest and elsewhere in Germany and reaching Czechoslovakia by the end of the war. The 3rd Ranger Battalion was formed in North Africa with some 1st Rangers as a basis and saw action in Sicily and Italy. The 4th Ranger Battalion was formed in May 1943, and saw service in Sicily and Italy. The 5th Ranger Battalion was formed in September 1943, and took part in the D-Day landings. Assigned to Patton's Third Army, the 5th Rangers carried out recon missions ahead of advancing US forces. Rangers from the battalion infiltrated and scouted ahead during the Third Army breakout from Normandy. After the liberation of Buchenwald concentration camp, Patton assigned Rangers the task of "escorting" Germans to see the camp. As Patton advanced into Austria, the 5th Rangers seized a bridge across the Danube. The 6th Ranger Battalion was formed in August 1944, on New Guinea. The best-known mission carried out by the 6th Rangers was the rescue of American PoWs from the Cabanatuan Prison Camp in the Philippines on January 30, 1945.

1st Special Service Force

The 1st Special Service Force was one of the most highly trained special forces units of World War II. Initially formed in June 1942, to carry out sabotage missions and raids in occupied Norway using "Weasel" tracked vehicles, Force members were eventually trained in parachuting, skiing, mountaineering, and amphibious operations. The joint US and Canadian unit recruited heavily among outdoorsmen, lumberjacks, trappers, professional hunters, and others with experience of living in the wild. Eventually, the Force fought in Italy during the advance on Rome and in the "Champagne campaign" in the South of France. The unit suffered heavy casualties and survivors were eventually incorporated into a regular infantry unit in January 1945. Today's US Special Forces trace their lineage to the 1st Special Service Force.

FURTHER READING

Alexander, Joseph H. *Edson's Raiders: The 1st Marine Raider Battalion in World War II*. Annapolis, MD: Naval Institute Press (2001)

Brett, Homer M. *The Military Knife and Bayonet*. Tokyo: World Photo Press (2001)

Brunner, Dr John W. *OSS Weapons*. Williamstown, NJ: Phillips Publications (1994)

Buerlein, Robert A. *Allied Military Fighting Knives and the Men Who Made Them Famous*. Richmond, VA: American Historical Foundation (1984)

Cassidy, W.L. *Quick or Dead*. Boulder, CO: Paladin Press, 1994

Cherry, Niall. *Striking Back: Britain's Airborne and Commando Raids, 1940–42*. Solihull: Helion and Company (2009)

Fairbairn, W.E. *Get Tough! How to Win in Hand-to-Hand Fighting*. Boulder, CO: Paladin Press (1979. Originally published 1942)

Fairbairn, W.E. *Scientific Self-Defense*. San Francisco: Interservice Publishing (1981)

Flook, Ron. *British and Commonwealth Military Knives*. Shrewsbury: Airlife (1999)

Hampshire, A. Cecil. *The Beachhead Commandos*. London: Kimber (1983)

Holman, Gordon. *Commando Attack*. London: Hodder & Stoughton, Ltd (1942)

Hughes, Gordon, Jenkins, Barry, and Buerlein, Robert A. *Knives of War: A Guide to Military Knives From World War II to the Present*. Boulder, CO: Paladin Press (2006)

Hunt, Robert E. *Randall Fighting Knives in Wartime: WWII, Korea, and Vietnam*. Paducah, KY: Turner Publishing (2002)

James, Malcolm. *Born of the Desert*. London: Collins (1945)

Ladd, James. *Commandos and Rangers of World War II*. London: Macdonald and Janes (1978)

Ladd, James & Melton, Keith. *Clandestine Warfare: Weapons and Equipment of the SOE and OSS*. London: Blandford Press (1988)

Lee, David. *Beachhead Assault: The Story of the Royal Naval Commandos in World War II*. London: Greenhill Books (2004)

Lodwick, John. *The Filibusters: The Story of the Special Boat Service*. London: Methuen, Ltd (1947)

Melton, H. Keith. *Ultimate Spy*. London: DK (2002)

Michel, Wolfgang. Das Fairbairn-Sykes Kampfmesser: Symbol britischer Guerillakriegsführung im Zweiten Weltkrieg. Norderstedt: Herstellung und Verlag (2007)

O'Donnell, Patrick K. *Operators, Spies, and Saboteurs: The Unknown Story of the Men and Women of WWII's OSS*. New York: Free Press (2004)

Smith, George W. *Carlson's Raid: The Daring Marine Assault on Makin*. Novato, CA: Presidio (2001)

Springer, Joseph A. *The Black Devil Brigade: The True Story of the First Special Service Force – An Oral History*. Pacifica, CA: Pacifica Military History (2004)

Stephens, Frederick J. *Fighting Knives: An Illustrated Guide to Fighting Knives and Military Survival Weapons of the World*. London: Arms and Armour Press (1980)

Thompson, Leroy. *Commando Dagger: The Complete Illustrated History of the Fairbairn-Sykes Fighting Knife*. Boulder, CO: Paladin Press (1985)

Thompson, Leroy. *Survival/Fighting Knives*. Boulder, CO: Paladin Press (1986)

Thompson, Leroy. *British Commandos in Action*. Carrollton, TX: Squadron/Signal (1987)

Trenowden, Ian. *Stealthily by Night: The COPPists Clandestine Beach Reconnaissance and Operations in World War II*. Crecy Books Ltd (1995)

Wellsted, Ian. *SAS with the Maquis: In Action with the French Resistance, June–September, 1944*. London: Greenhill Books (1997)

Wickersham, Sheldon & Edna. *Randall Knives: A Reference Book*. Published by the authors (2007)

Wilkinson-Latham, Robert. *Wilkinsons and the F-S Fighting Knife*. Shoreham-by-Sea: Pooley Sword Publishing (2009)

Windrum, Dr William. *Clandestine Edged Weapons*. Williamstown, NJ: Phillips Publications (1991)

Windrum, Dr William. *The Earliest Commando Knives*. Williamstown, NJ: Phillips Publications (1991)

INDEX

Numbers in bold refer to images.